# Tesla in His Own Words

Wisdom from one of the world's greatest inventors

~

# Tako je govorio Tesla

Mudrosti jednog od najvećih svetskih pronalazača

*Dobrica Savić*

Cataloguing in Publication Data

Names: Savić, Dobrica, 1956- author. | Kunz, Rebecca, editor of English text. | Savić
Lopičić, Marija, illustrator. | Savić, Bojan, cover designer.
Title: Tesla in his own words : wisdom from one of the world's greatest inventors /
Dobrica Savić.
Other title : Tako je govorio Tesla : Mudrosti jednog od najvećih svetskih pronalazača
Description: Vienna : Independently published, ©2019.
Identifiers: ISBN 978–107335029 (paperback)
Subjects: LCSH: Tesla, Nikola, 1856-1943. | Inventors — Croatia. | Quotations.
Classification: UDC 5-051(082.2).

# Contents / Sadržaj

# Tesla in His Own Words

### Wisdom from one of the world's greatest inventors

Dedicated to all who believe that knowledge, combined with inspiration and hard work, can make the world a much better place.

It seems that I have always been ahead of my time.

*Nikola Tesla*

# Nikola Tesla
## Short Biography

**Nikola Tesla** is considered one of the world's greatest inventors. An electrical engineer, mechanical engineer, physicist, and futurist, he is best known for designing the modern alternating current (AC) electricity supply system. For many, he was regarded as a genius who lit up and electrified the world, a modern Prometheus, one of the greatest scientists in history. A true visionary whose inventions continue to live on.

Tesla was born on July 10, 1856 in the village of Smiljan, near Gospić (a small town in the Austro-Hungarian Empire), to Milutin Tesla, a priest of the Serbian Orthodox Church, and his wife Georgina (Djuka) Tesla (née Mandić), whose father was also a Serbian Orthodox priest.

Tesla attended elementary school in Smiljan, junior high school in Gospić, and high school in Karlovac. The idea of making an AC motor, without commutators and brushes, first occurred to Tesla in 1877 during his second year at Graz's Polytechnic School while attending a lecture by Professor Poeschl. Poeschl gave a demonstration of a dynamo operating as a motor. Noticing sparks emitting from the dynamo, Tesla believed it would be possible to create a dynamo that didn't lose as much energy by using alternating current. Although laughed at for this ridiculous idea, Tesla obsessed on the notion that it could be done. Professor Poeschl was aware of Tesla's genius and noted that "Nikola's ability at mathematics is phenomenal. He knows the answers as quickly as the professor puts the problems on the board. He figures the answers out mentally and hardly ever writes the problem down". [https://teslaresearch.jimdo.com/biography-1856-1943/]

In 1880, Tesla went to Prague to study natural philosophy at Charles University. In 1881, he started work as an electrician at a telephone company in Budapest. It was here that he came up with the idea for an induction motor. Travelling to Paris, he hoped to sell his idea to the Continental Edison Company, but they were not interested in alternating current. However, he persisted and in 1883 built his first induction motor. He decided to try his luck in America with Edison, hoping the climate would be more conducive to accepting AC.

At age 28, Nikola Tesla arrived in New York City with four cents in his pocket, some mathematical computations, a drawing of an idea for a flying machine, and a letter of introduction from Charles Batchelor, one of Edison's business associates in Europe. Upon his first glimpse of New York, the Serbian immigrant was shocked by what he observed. "What I had left was beautiful, artistic and fascinating in every way; what I saw here was machined, rough and unattractive. It [America] is a century behind Europe in civilization." Edison sensed something special about Tesla and hired him immediately to make improvements in his DC generation plants. However, claimed it was a joke, Edison reneged on his offer of $50,000 for Tesla to solve a number of engineering problems and Tesla quit the company. He reportedly dug ditches for a year. Eventually he formed the Tesla Electric Company and received an upfront payment plus royalties after Westinghouse made arrangements to license the technology for his AC induction motor.

Tesla was a workaholic, often working 18-hour days. Even into old age, Tesla slept only two or three hours a night. He was known not only for his scientific and engineering accomplishments but also for his personal phobias, rituals, and beliefs. One of them was his obsession with numbers, in particular the numbers 3, 6 and 9. He used to say that, "if you only knew the magnificence of the 3, 6 and 9, then you would have a key to the universe".

With his inventions, Tesla possibly contributed more than any other scientist worldwide. He invented the alternating current used today, and the way light is harnessed and distributed. He used fluorescent bulbs in his lab 40 years before they were actually 'invented'. It was Tesla who invented the radio, not Marconi — who in fact received a Nobel prize for that invention. He demonstrated a 'teleautomaton' device, a robotic boat controlled by radio waves. His invention of the induction motor was incredibly influential and is still used in industry and in household gadgets such as vacuums, fans, and power tools.

Tesla held at least 308 patents from 27 countries on five continents. Most of them — 116 — were registered in the United States. 126 were basic patents for inventions registered for the first time, while the rest were equivalent patents, registering the same invention to protect them in different countries. Throughout his rich scientific career, Tesla discovered, designed and developed ideas for a number of important inventions — most of which were officially patented by other inventors.

Tesla was a technical and visionary genius. He probed deeply into the secrets of nature, allowing us to benefit from his inventions.

Nikola Tesla died alone on January 7, 1943, at the age of 86, in New York City, where he had lived for nearly 60 years.

# Tesla's wisdoms from A to W

# Achievement

⚡ From childhood I was compelled to concentrate attention upon myself. This caused me much suffering, but to my present view, it was a blessing in disguise for it has taught me to appreciate the inestimable value of introspection in the preservation of life, as well as a means of achievement.

## Aim

⚡ Do not strike at what you are looking but at what you intend to hit.

# Airplanes

⚡ I do not hesitate to state here for future reference and as a test of the accuracy of my scientific forecast that flying machines and ships propelled by electricity transmitted without wire will have ceased to be a wonder in ten years from now. I would say five were it not that there is such a thing as "inertia of human opinion" resisting revolutionary ideas.

# Archimedes

⚡ Archimedes was my ideal.

# Artificial intelligence

⚡ Mechanisms can be produced which will act as if possest of reason, to a limited degree, and will create a revolution in many commercial and industrial departments.

# Books

⚡ Of all things I liked books the best.

⚡ On one occasion I started to read the works of Voltaire when I learned, to my dismay, that there were close on one hundred large volumes in small print which that monster had written while drinking seventy-two cups of black coffee per diem. It had to be done, but when I laid aside the last book I was very glad, and said, "Never more!"

# Camphor

⚡ If a piece of camphor was anywhere in the house it caused me the keenest discomfort.

# Carrier

⚡ By an irony of fate, my first employment was as a draughtsman. I hated drawing; it was for me the very worst of annoyances. Fortunately, it was not long before I secured the position I sought, that of chief electrician to the telephone company.

# Childhood

⚡ From my childhood I had been intended for the clergy. This prospect hung like a dark cloud on my mind.

# Civilization

⚡ The spread of civilization may be likened to a fire; first, a feeble spark, next a flickering flame, then a mighty blaze, ever increasing in speed and power.

# Crystals

⚡ Crystals are living beings at the beginning of creation.

⚡ In crystal we have a pure evidence of the existence of a formative life principle, and although in spite of everything we cannot understand the life of crystals — it is still a living being.

# Desire

⚡ When natural inclination develops into a passionate desire, one advances towards his goal in seven-league boots.

# Destiny

⚡ As I review the events of my past life I realize how subtle are the influences that shape our destinies.

# Destruction

⚡ To conquer the steep force becomes more and more difficult every day. Defense is a continuous obtaining the advantages of attack, as if we make progress in the sotonic science of destruction.

⚡ We build but to tear down. Most of our work and resource is squandered. Our onward march is marked by devastation. Everywhere there is an appalling loss of time, effort and life. A cheerless view, but true.

# Disruptor

⚡ It is a radical departure in the sense that its success would mean the abandonment of the antiquated types of prime movers on which billions of dollars have been spent.

# Dreams

⚡ Someday, but not at this time, I shall make an announcement of something that I never once dreamed of.

# Earrings

⚡ I had a violent aversion against the earrings of women but other ornaments, [*sic*] as bracelets, pleased me more or less according to design.

# Earth

⚡ The earth may explode. A planet may collide with us. Yet it has existed a long time.

⚡ The issue of great importance shall be to know: what is the capacity of Earth? And what is the charge if it is electrified?

⚡ The idea gradually took hold of me that the earth might be used in place of the wire, thus dispensing with artificial conductors altogether. The immensity of the globe seemed an unsurmountable obstacle but after a prolonged study of the subject I became satisfied that the undertaking was rational.

# Electrical power

⚡ But among all these many departments of research, these many branches of industry, new and old, which are being rapidly expanded, there is one dominating all others in importance — one which is of the greatest significance for the comfort and welfare, not to say for the existence, of mankind, and that is the electrical transmission of power.

⚡ Electric power is everywhere present in unlimited quantities and can drive the world's machinery without the need for coal, oil, or gas.

## Electrical science

⚡ Electrical science has disclosed to us the more intimate relation existing between widely different forces and phenomena and has thus led us to a more complete comprehension of Nature and its many manifestations to our senses.

⚡ Electrical science has revealed to us the true nature of light, has provided us with innumerable appliances and instruments of precision, and has thereby vastly added to the exactness of our knowledge.

⚡ Of the various branches of electrical investigation, perhaps the most interesting and immediately the most promising is that dealing with alternating currents.

⚡ So astounding are the facts in this connection, that it would seem as though the Creator, Himself had electrically designed this planet.

## Electricity

⚡ As in nature, all is ebb and tide, all is wave motion, so it seems that in all branches of industry, alternating currents — electric wave motion — will have the sway.

⚡ The day when we shall know exactly what "electricity" is, will chronicle an event probably greater, more important than any other recorded in the history of the human race. The time will come when the comfort, the very existence, perhaps, of man will depend upon that wonderful agent.

⚡ The feeling is constantly growing on me that I had been the first to hear the greeting of one planet to another.

⚡ This planet, with all its appalling immensity, is to electric currents virtually no more than a small metal ball.

⚡ We wind a simple ring of iron with coils; we establish the connections to the generator, and with wonder and delight we note the effects of strange forces which we bring into play, which allow us to transform, to transmit and direct energy at will.

⚡ Now, I must tell you of a strange experience which bore fruit in my later life. We had a cold [snap] drier than even observed before. People walking in the snow left a luminous trail. [As I stroked] cat's back, a sheet of light [came] and my hand produced a shower of sparks. My father remarked, this is nothing but electricity, the same thing you see on the trees in a storm. My mother seemed alarmed. Stop playing with the cat, she said, he might start a fire. I was thinking abstractly. Is nature a cat? If so, who strokes its back? It can only be God, I concluded. I cannot exaggerate the effect of this marvelous sight on my childish imagination. Day after day I asked myself what is electricity and found no answer. Eighty years have gone by since and I still ask the same question, unable to answer it.

# Energy

⚡ There is no energy in matter other than that received from the environment.

⚡ It is absolutely impossible to convert mass into energy.

⚡ We are whirling through endless space, with an inconceivable speed, all around everything is spinning, everything is moving, everywhere there is energy. There must be some way of availing ourselves of this energy more directly. Then, with the light obtained from the medium, with the power derived from it, with every form of energy obtained without effort, from the store forever inexhaustible, humanity will advance with giant strides. The mere contemplation of these magnificent possibilities expand our minds, strengthens our hopes and fills our hearts with supreme delight.

⚡ Throughout space there is energy. Is this energy static or kinetic! If static our hopes are in vain; if kinetic — and this we know it is, for certain — then it is a mere question of time when men will succeed in attaching their machinery to the very wheelwork of nature.

⚡ But we shall not satisfy ourselves simply with improving steam and explosive engines or inventing new batteries; we have something much better to work for, a greater task to fulfill. We have to evolve means for obtaining energy from stores which are forever inexhaustible, to perfect methods which do not imply consumption and waste of any material whatever.

# Extraterrestrial life

⚡ Most certainly, some planets are not inhabited, but others are, and among these there must exist life under all conditions and phases of development.

⚡ If there are intelligent inhabitants of Mars or any other planet, it seems to me that we can do something to attract their attention... I have had this scheme under consideration for five or six years.

13

⚡ My ear barely caught signals coming in regular succession which could not have been produced on earth.

⚡ There must be life on other planets. The sun shines. The stars give out heat. Water collects on the surface. Chemical changes occur that we do not yet understand — and there is life.

# Feelings

⚡ One may feel a sudden wave of sadness and rake his brain for an explanation when he might have noticed that it was caused by a cloud cutting off the rays of the sun.

# Food

⚡ There is no doubt that some plant food, such as oatmeal, is more economical than meat, and superior to it in regard to both mechanical and mental performance. Such food, moreover, taxes our digestive organs decidedly less, and, in making us more contented and sociable, produces an amount of good difficult to estimate.

# Forgiveness

⚡ On more than one occasion you have offended me, but in my qualities both as Christian and philosopher I have always forgiven you and only pitied you for your errors.

# Freedom

⚡ The vast majority of human beings are not observant sufficiently that they live in the illusion of perfect choice and freedom in their thoughts and actions.

# Frequency

⚡ All things have a frequency and a vibration.

# Future

⚡ Let the future tell the truth and evaluate each one according to his work and accomplishments. The present is theirs, the future, for which I really worked, is mine.

⚡ The discovery of a new scientific truth will be more important than the squabbles of diplomats.

⚡ The individual will not be permitted to achieve great wealth and power; his privacy will be invaded in a thousand ways. He will be restricted in his efforts in every direction — will virtually disappear in the wave of collectivism which will sweep the world.

⚡ This materialistic tide can only be stemmed by idealism, which is a force tending to free what we call the soul of man from physical fetters. But although there might be periods of alternating dominance of these two principles — materialism and idealism — ultimately the materialistic tendencies will become dominating.

⚡ Today the most civilized countries of the world spend a maximum of their income on war and a minimum on education. The twenty-first century will reverse this order.

⚡ The future will show whether my foresight is as accurate now as it has proved heretofore.

# Gambling

⚡ I have been as indifferent to any form of gambling as to picking teeth.

# God

⚡ The gift of mental power comes from God, Divine Being, and if we concentrate our minds on that truth, we become in tune with this great power.

⚡ We are inspired both by Christianity and Science to do our utmost toward increasing the performance of mankind.

⚡ What one man calls God, another calls the laws of physics.

# Hair

⚡ I would not touch the hair of other people except, perhaps, at the point of a revolver.

# Hate

⚡ If your hate could be turned into electricity, it would light up the whole world.

# Horrors

⚡ You may live to see man-made horrors beyond your comprehension.

# Humanity

⚡ There is something within me that might be illusion as it is often the case with young delighted people, but if I would be fortunate to achieve some of my ideals, it would be on the behalf of the whole of humanity.

⚡ The progress and development of man are of immeasurable importance for humanity and are essentially dependent on invention.

# Humans

⚡ Everyone should consider his body as a priceless gift from one whom he loves above all, a marvelous work of art, of indescribable beauty, and mystery beyond human conception, and so delicate that a word, a breath, a look, nay, a thought may injure it.

⚡ Our senses enable us to perceive only a minute portion of the outside world.

⚡ Our virtues and our failings are inseparable, like force and matter. When they separate, man is no more.

⚡ The human being is a self-propelled automaton entirely under the control of external influences. Willful and predetermined though they appear, his actions are governed not from within, but from without. He is like a float tossed about by the waves of a turbulent sea.

⚡ Though free to think and act, we are held together, like the stars in the firmament, with ties inseparable. These ties cannot be seen, but we can feel them.

# Hydro power

⚡ We have many a monument of past ages; we have the palaces and pyramids, the temples of the Greek and the cathedrals of Christendom. In them is exemplified the power of men, the greatness of nations, the love of art and religious devotion. But the monument at Niagara has something of its own, more in accord with our present thoughts and tendencies. It is a monument worthy of our scientific age, a true monument of enlightenment and of peace. It signifies the subjugation of natural forces to the service of man, the discontinuance of barbarous methods, the relieving of millions from want and suffering.

# Idea

⚡ A new idea must not be judged by its immediate results.

⚡ Be alone, that is the secret of invention; be alone, that is when ideas are born.

⚡ I don't care that they stole my idea ... I care that they don't have any of their own.

⚡ New ideas are adopted gradually. It is inevitable that those who are in the forefront of the advance will keep their places. Our life is now so regulated that no advance whatever could completely upset the existing order.

⚡ The carrying out into practice of a crude idea as is being generally done is, I hold, nothing but a waste of energy, money and time.

⚡ The practical success of an idea, irrespective of inherent possibilities, depends on the attitude of contemporaries.

⚡ With ideas it is like with dizzy heights you climb: At first, they cause you discomfort and you are anxious to get down, distrustful of your own powers; but soon the remoteness of the turmoil of life and the inspiring influence of the altitude calm your blood; your step gets firm and sure and you begin to look – for dizzier heights.

# Ideals

⚡ The struggle for existence being lessened, there should be development along ideal rather than material lines.

⚡ We must all have some ideal which will govern our behaviour and satisfy us, but it is not material. It can be religion, art, science, whatever, it is only important that it acts as a non-material force.

# Ignorance

⚡ Deficient observation is merely a form of ignorance and responsible for the many morbid notions and foolish ideas prevailing.

⚡ It is paradoxical, yet true, to say, that the more we know, the more ignorant we become in the absolute sense, for it is only through enlightenment that we become conscious of our limitations. Precisely one of the most gratifying results of intellectual evolution is the continuous opening up of new and greater prospects.

⚡ It will be more glorious to fight against ignorance than to die on the field of battle.

⚡ Of all the frictional resistances, the one that most retards human movement is ignorance, what Buddha called 'the greatest evil in the world'. The friction which results from ignorance can be reduced only by the spread of knowledge and the unification of the heterogeneous elements of humanity. No effort could be better spent.

# Imagination

⚡ Our first strivings are exclusively the instinctive stimulus of lively imagination and non-discipline.

⚡ When I get an idea I start at once building it up in my imagination. I change the construction, make improvements and operate the device in my mind. It is absolutely immaterial to me whether I run my turbine in thought or test it in my shop.

⚡ I predict that very shortly the old-fashioned incandescent lamp, having a filament heated to brightness by the passage of electric current through it, will entirely disappear.

# Instinct

⚡ Instinct is something which transcends knowledge. We have, undoubtedly, certain finer fibers that enable us to perceive truths when logical deduction, or any other willful effort of the brain, is futile.

⚡ Our first endeavors are purely instinctive, promptings of an imagination vivid and undisciplined. As we grow older reason asserts itself and we become more and more systematic and designing. But those early impulses, though not immediately productive, are of the greatest moment and may shape our very destinies. Indeed, I feel now that had I understood and cultivated instead of suppressing them, I would have added substantial value to my bequest to the world.

# Intelligence

⚡ My conviction has grown so strong that I no longer look on this plan of energy or intelligence transmission as a mere theoretical possibility, but as a serious problem in electrical engineering, which must be carried out some day.

# Introspection

⚡ Appreciate the inestimable value of introspection in the preservation of life.

⚡ It is a common mistake to avoid imaginary and ignore the real dangers.

⚡ Nothing enters our minds or determines our actions which is not directly or indirectly a response to stimuli beating upon our sense organs from without.

⚡ Most persons are so absorbed in the contemplation of the outside world that they are wholly oblivious to what is passing on within themselves.

# Invention

⚡ I do not think there is any thrill that can go through the human heart like that felt by the inventor as he sees some creation of the brain unfolding to success... Such emotions make a man forget food, sleep, friends, love, everything.

⚡ I do not think you can name many great inventions that have been made by married men.

⚡ I have hundreds of inventions which I could not take the patents of, on account of my misfortune.

⚡ Invention is the most important product of man's creative brain. The ultimate purpose is the complete mastery of mind over the material world, the harnessing of human nature to human needs.

⚡ Inventors don't have time for married life.

⚡ My method is different. I do not rush into actual work. When I get a new idea, I start at once building it up in my imagination and make improvements and operate the device in my mind. When I have gone so far as to embody everything in my invention, every possible improvement I can think of, and when I see no fault anywhere, I put into concrete form the final product of my brain.

⚡ Perhaps it is better in this present world of ours that a revolutionary idea or invention instead of being helped and patted, be hampered and ill-treated in its adolescence.

⚡ The progressive development of man is vitally dependent on invention. It is the most important product of his creative brain.

# Inventor

⚡ I admired the works of artists, but to my mind, they were only shadows and semblances. The inventor, I thought, gives to the world creations which are palpable, which live and work.

⚡ If this does not appeal to you sufficiently to recognize in me a discoverer of principles, do me, at least, the justice of calling me an "inventor of some beautiful pieces of electrical apparatus."

⚡ Not until I had attained manhood did I realize that I was an inventor.

⚡ The inventor finds a huge compensation in the pleasure offered by his work and in knowing that he is an individual of extraordinary capabilities without whom our species would long be extinct in the fierce struggle against merciless elements.

# Knowledge

⚡ All knowledge or form conception is evoked through the medium of the eye, either in response to disturbances directly received on the retina or to their fainter secondary effects and reverberations. Other sense organs can only call forth feelings which have no reality of existence and of which no conception can be formed.

⚡ If the genius of invention were to reveal tomorrow the secret of immortality, of eternal beauty and youth, for which all humanity is aching, the same inexorable agents which prevent a mass from changing suddenly its velocity would likewise resist the force of the new knowledge until time gradually modifies human thought.

⚡ The danger of conflict increases dangerously because of a more or less dominant feeling of belligerency which is present in every human being. The best way to oppose this tendency is to dispel the ignorance by a systematic spreading of general knowledge. Bearing this in mind the most important is help through an exchange of opinions and relations.

# Language

⚡ I felt that the time I had spent studying languages, literature and art was wasted; though later, of course, I learned this was not so.

⚡ I learned a dozen languages, studied literature and arts, spent my best years in libraries reading everything that came my way, and though I sometimes felt I was losing time, I quickly realized it was the best thing I ever did.

⚡ Mutual understanding will be infinitely easier by the use of one universal language.

# Laziness

⚡ I do not believe in laziness, and I should like to see the loafer wiped from the face or [*sic*] the earth; but I want that those who are willing to work should accomplish their results with the least labor and in the best way.

# Leisure

⚡ Too much leisure, and civilization will go to pot.

# Life

⚡ Life was inevitable.

⚡ Life is and will ever remain an equation incapable of solution, but it contains certain known factors.

⚡ The opinion of the world does not affect me. I have placed as the real values in my life what follows when I am dead.

⚡ Of all the endless variety of phenomena which nature presents to our senses, there is none that fills our mind with greater wonder than that inconceivably complex movement which … we designate as human life. Its mysterious origin is veiled in the forever impenetrable mist of the past, its character is rendered incomprehensible by its infinite intricacy, and its destination is hidden in the unfathomable depths of the future.

⚡ Even matter which is called inorganic, deemed dead, responds to the disbelievers and gives irrefutable proof of the living principle within itself. Everything that exists, organic or inorganic, living and non-living is sensitive to outside stimuli.

⚡ I come from a very wiry and long-lived race. Some of my ancestors have been centenarians, and one of them lived 129 years. I am determined to keep up the record and please myself with prospects of great promise. Then again, nature has given me a vivid imagination.

# Love

⚡ It's not the love you make. It's the love you give.

# Man

⚡ I see a friend hurt, and it hurts me, too: my friend and I are one.… we are all one.

⚡ I was merely an automaton endowed with power of movement, responding to the stimuli of the sense organs and thinking and acting accordingly.

⚡ Man, like the universe, is a machine.

⚡ The individual is ephemeral, races and nations come and pass away, but man remains. Therein lies the profound difference between the individual and the whole.

⚡ To cause at will the birth and death of matter would be man's grandest deed, which would give him the mastery of physical creation, make him fulfill his ultimate destiny.

# Mankind

⚡ The desire that guides me in all I do is the desire to harness the forces of nature to the service of mankind.

# Marconi

⚡ Marconi is a good fellow. Let him continue. He is using seventeen of my patents.

# Mark Twain

⚡ One day I was handed a few volumes of new literature unlike anything I had ever read before and so captivating as to make me utterly forget my hopeless state. They were the earlier works of Mark Twain and to them might have been due the miraculous recovery which followed. Twenty-five years later, when I met Mr. Clemens and we formed a friendship between us, I told him of the experience and was amazed to see that great man of laughter burst into tears.

# Mathematics

⚡ There is scarcely a subject that cannot be mathematically treated and the effects calculated or the results determined beforehand from the available theoretical and practical data.

# Mental powers

⚡ The incessant mental exertion developed my powers of observation and enabled me to discover a truth of great importance.

# Mind

⚡ Man must exercise temperance and control of his senses and leanings in every way, thus keeping himself young in body and mind.

⚡ The ultimate purpose is the complete mastery of mind over the material world, the harnessing of human nature to human needs.

⚡ The mind is sharper and keener in seclusion and uninterrupted solitude. No big laboratory is needed in which to think. Originality thrives in seclusion free of outside influences beating upon us to cripple the creative mind.

⚡ How extraordinary was my life an incident may illustrate... [as a youth] I was fascinated by a description of Niagara Falls I had perused and pictured in my imagination a big wheel run by the Falls. I told my uncle that I would go to America and carry out this scheme. Thirty years later I saw my ideas carried out at Niagara and marveled at the unfathomable mystery of the mind.

# Mindfulness

⚡ The perfect purity of the air, the unequaled beauty of the sky, the imposing sight of a high mountain range, the quiet and restfulness of the place — all around contributed to make the conditions for scientific observation ideal.

# Misunderstandings

⚡ Fights between individuals, as well as governments and nations, invariably result from misunderstandings in the broadest interpretation of this term. Misunderstandings are always caused by the inability of appreciating one another's point of view.

# Money

⚡ Money does not represent such a value as men have placed upon it. All my money has been invested into experiments with which I have made new discoveries enabling mankind to have a little easier life.

⚡ No desire for material advantages has animated me in all this work, though I hope, for the sake of the continuance of my labors, that these will soon follow, naturally, as a compensation for valuable services rendered to science and industry.

⚡ The technical advances are inevitably driving us toward the grossest kind of materialism. And it will not be very long before the social system of bee life will become universal.

# Moral

⚡ Scientific developments may even affect our morals and customs.

# Music

⚡ I am part of a light, and it is the music. Particles of Light are written note. O bolt of lightning can be an entire sonata. A thousand balls of lightening is a concert.

# Nature

⚡ A single ray of light from a distant star falling upon the eye of a tyrant in bygone times may have altered the course of his life, may have changed the destiny of nations, may have transformed the surface of the globe, so intricate, so inconceivably complex are the processes in Nature.

⚡ I would give a thousand secrets of nature upon which I stumbled by accident, in exchange for this one which I extracted from nature, in spite of all the miracles and dangers which I faced.

⚡ If you don't know how, observe the phenomena of nature, they will give you clear answers and inspiration.

⚡ In no way can we get such an overwhelming idea of the grandeur of Nature than when we consider, that in accordance with the law of the conservation of energy, throughout the Infinite, the forces are in a perfect balance, and hence the energy of a single thought may determine the motion of a universe.

⚡ It is quite evident, though, that this squandering cannot go on indefinitely, for geological investigations prove our fuel stores to be limited. So great has been the drain on them of late years that the specter of exhaustion is looming up threateningly in the distance

⚡ The history of science shows that theories are perishable.

⚡ With every new truth that is revealed we get a better understanding of Nature and our conceptions and views are modified.

# New world

⚡ A new world must be born, a world that would justify the sacrifices offered by humanity. This new world must be a world in which there shall be no exploitation of the weak by the strong, of the good by the evil; where there will be no humiliation of the poor by the violence of the rich; where the products of intellect, science and art will serve society for the betterment and beautification of life, and not the individuals for achieving wealth. This new world shall not be a world of the downtrodden and humiliated, but of free men and free nations, equal in dignity and respect.

# Observation

⚡ Insufficient observation is only a form of unknowing, a cause of many perverse incidents and a triumph of crazy ideas.

# Opportunity

⚡ Great moments are born great opportunity.

# Patience

⚡ If I were to try every crude idea when it first came into my mind I could 'bust' two banks every day. That is the trouble with many inventors; they lack patience. They lack the willingness to work a thing out slowly and clearly and sharply in their mind, so that they can actually 'feel it work.' They want to try their first idea right off; and the result is they use up lots of money and lots of good material, only to find eventually that they are working in the wrong direction. We all make mistakes, and it is better to make them before we begin.

# Patriotism

⚡ As long as there are different nationalities, there will be patriotism. That feeling has to be rooted out from our hearts before the permanent peace is established. It should be replaced by love towards nature and scientific ideal. Science and inventions are strong forces which will lead to its termination.

# Peace

⚡ Peace can only come as a natural consequence of universal enlightenment and merging of races, and we are still far from this blissful realization.

⚡ What we now want is closer contact and better understanding between individuals and communities all over the earth, and the elimination of egoism and pride which is always prone to plunge the world into primeval barbarism and strife.

⚡ The greatest value of my invention will result from its effect upon warfare and armaments, for by reason of its certain and unlimited destructiveness it will tend to bring about and maintain permanent peace among nations.

⚡ The universal peace as a result of cumulative efforts through the centuries can come into being quickly — not like crystal which at once forms a solution that has been slowly in preparation.

# Peach

⚡ I would get a fever by looking at a peach.

## Pearls

⚡ The sight of a pearl would almost give me a fit but I was fascinated with the glitter of crystals or objects with sharp edges and plane surfaces.

## People

⚡ We are all one. People are interconnected by invisible forces. Although we have the freedom to think and act, we stick together, like stars on the heavenly arc, with unbreakable connections. These connections cannot be seen, but we can feel them.

## Pigeons

⚡ I have been feeding pigeons, thousands of them for years. But there was one, a beautiful bird, pure white with light grey tips on its wings; that one was different. It was a female. I had only to wish and call her and she would come flying to me. I loved that pigeon as a man loves a woman, and she loved me. As long as I had her, there was a purpose to my life.

# Political alliances

⚡ These are only new devices for putting the weak at the mercy of the strong.

# Poverty

⚡ If we want to reduce poverty and misery, if we want to give to every deserving individual what is needed for a safe existence of an intelligent being, we want to provide more machinery, more power. Power is our mainstay, the primary source of our many-sided energies.

# Progress

⚡ Human activity has become so widespread and intense that years count as centuries of progress. There is no more groping in the dark or accidentally stumbling upon discoveries. The results follow one another like the links of a chain. Such is the force of the accumulated knowledge and the insight into natural laws and phenomena that future events are clearly projected before our vision.

# Privacy

⚡ Perhaps we shall shortly get so used to this state of things that nobody will feel the slightest embarrassment while he is conscious that his skeleton and other particulars are being scrutinized by indelicate observers.

# Providence

⚡ Very probably my career would have ended ahead of its time if Providence did not provide me with a defence mechanism which got stronger year by year and which unerringly activated itself whenever my forces were at their end.

# Radio

⚡ I know I'm its father, but I just don't like it. It's a nuisance. I never listen to it. The radio is a distraction and keeps you from concentrating.

# Reason

⚡ As we grow older reason asserts itself and we become more and more systematic and designing.

# Reading

⚡ Whenever I could manage I tried to satisfy my passion for reading.

# Religion

⚡ There is no conflict between the ideal of religion and the ideal of science, but science is opposed to theological dogmas because science is founded on fact.

# Rewards

⚡ Restraint has not always been according to my taste, but my pleasurable experiences are a huge reward.

⚡ The true rewards are ever in proportion to the labor and sacrifices made.

# Robots

⚡ In the twenty-first century, the robot will take the place which slave labor occupied in ancient civilization.

# Rotating field

⚡ I would not give my rotating field discovery for a thousand inventions, however valuable... A thousand years hence, the telephone and the motion picture camera may be obsolete, but the principle of the rotating magnetic field will remain a vital, living thing for all time to come.

# Salvation

⚡ One's salvation could only be brought about through his own efforts.

# Science

⚡ Science and inventions are strong forces which will lead to its termination.

⚡ Science is a personal perversion except if its end goal is the betterment of mankind.

⚡ Science is opposed to theological dogmas because science is founded on fact.

⚡ If two planets collide at [*sic*] certain time and certain place, this is to the student of positive science an inevitable result of preceding interactions between the bodies; and if our knowledge would be adequate, we would be able to foretell the event accurately.

# Scientist

⚡ A scientist is not aiming toward sudden results. He does not expect his advanced ideas to be readily accepted.

⚡ Humanity is not yet sufficiently advanced to be willingly led by the discoverer's keen searching sense.

⚡ The scientific man does not aim at an immediate result. He does not expect that his advanced ideas will be readily taken up. His work is like that of the planter — for the future. His duty is to lay the foundation for those who are to come and point the way. He lives and labors and hopes.

⚡ The scientists of today think deeply instead of clearly. One must be sane to think clearly, but one can think deeply and be quite insane.

⚡ Today's scientists have substituted mathematics for experiments, and they wander off through equation after equation, and eventually build a structure which has no relation to reality.

⚡ I have had but little time to devote to the fulfillment of a duty which, next to that of turning his best efforts to diligent inquiry in the fields he has chosen, is the most important to a scientific man; namely, that of giving an exact record of the results obtained

# Self-control

⚡ I conquered my weakness and felt a pleasure I never knew before — that of doing as I willed.

# Senses

⚡ Our senses enable us to perceive only minute parts of the outer world. Our debate takes place at a small distance. Our sight is obstructed by a wall and a shadow. In order to get to know one another we must circumvent the sphere of our feeling of perception.

# Serbians

⚡ Hardly is there a nation which has met with a sadder fate than the Serbians. From the height of its splendor, when the empire embraced almost the entire northern part of the Balkan peninsula and a large portion of what is now Austria, the Serbian nation was plunged into abject slavery, after the fateful battle of 1389 at the Kosovo Polje, against the overwhelming Asian hordes. Europe can never repay the great debt it owes to the Serbians for checking, by the sacrifice of its own liberty, that barbarian influx.

⚡ If I will have the luck to realize at least some of my ideas, it will be a benefaction for the whole mankind. If these hopes of mine come true, the sweetest thought will be that it is the work of a Serbian.

# Soul

⚡ In the course of ages, mechanisms of infinite complexity are developed, but what we call 'soul' or 'spirit,' is nothing more than the sum of the functionings of the body. When these [*sic*] functioning ceases, the 'soul' or the 'spirit' ceases likewise.

# Space

⚡ I hold that space cannot be curved, for the simple reason that it can have no properties.

⚡ To say that in the presence of large bodies space becomes curved is equivalent to stating that something can act upon nothing.

# Struggle

⚡ All that was great in the past was ridiculed, condemned, combated, suppressed — only to emerge all the more powerfully, all the more triumphantly from the struggle.

# Success

⚡ Every effort under compulsion demands a sacrifice of life-energy.

⚡ If I were ever assailed by doubt of ultimate success I would dismiss it by remembering the words of that great philosopher, Lord Kelvin, who after witnessing some of my experiments said to me with tears in his eyes: 'I am sure you will do it.'

⚡ It was the artist, too, who awakened that broad philanthropic spirit which, even in old ages, shone in the teachings of noble reformers and philosophers, that spirit which makes men in all departments and positions work not as much for any material benefit or compensation — though reason may command this also — but chiefly for the sake of success, for the pleasure there is in achieving it and for the good they might be able to do thereby to their fellow-men. Through his influence types of men are now pressing forward, impelled by a deep love for their study, men who are doing wonders in their respective branches, whose chief aim and enjoyment is the acquisition and spread of knowledge, men who look far above earthly things, whose banner is Excelsior! Gentlemen let us honor the artist; let us thank him, let us drink his health!

⚡ My project was retarded by laws of nature. The world was not prepared for it. It was too far ahead of time. But the same laws will prevail in the end and make it a triumphal success.

# Supernatural

⚡ The day science begins to study non-physical phenomena, it will make more progress in one decade than in all the previous centuries of its existence.

# Taste

⚡ When I drop little squares of paper in a dish filled with liquid, I always sense a peculiar and awful taste in my mouth.

# Telephone

⚡ When wireless is perfectly applied the whole earth will be converted into a huge brain, which in fact it is, all things being particles of a real and rhythmic whole. We shall be able to communicate with one another instantly, irrespective of distance. Not only this, but through television and telephony we shall see and hear one another as perfectly as though we were face to face, despite intervening distances of thousands of miles; and the instruments through which we shall be able to do this will be amazingly simple compared with our present telephone. A man will be able to carry one in his vest pocket.

⚡ With these developments we have every reason to anticipate that in a time not very distant most telegraphic messages across the oceans will be transmitted without cables. For short distances we need a 'wireless' telephone, which requires no expert operators.

# Thomas Edison

⚡ One of the great events in my life was my first meeting with Edison. This wonderful man, who had received no scientific training, yet had accomplished so much, filled me with amazement.

⚡ Edison was by far the most successful and, probably, the last exponent of the purely empirical method of investigation. Everything he achieved was the result of persistent trials and experiments often performed at random but always attesting extraordinary vigor and resource.

⚡ He had a veritable contempt for book learning and mathematical knowledge, trusting himself entirely to his inventor's instinct and practical American sense. In view of this, the truly prodigious amount of his actual accomplishments is little short of a miracle.

⚡ His existence was made up of alternate periods of work and sleep in the laboratory. He had no hobby, cared for no sport or amusement of any kind and lived in utter disregard of the most elementary rules of hygiene.
⚡ He will occupy a unique and exalted position in the history of his native land, which might well be proud of his great genius and undying achievements in the interest of humanity.

⚡ His mind was dominated by one idea, to leave no stone unturned, to exhaust every possibility.

⚡ I was amazed at this man, who, without thorough education or scientific experience did so much.

⚡ If he had a needle to find in a haystack, he would not stop to reason where it was most likely to be but would proceed at once with the feverish diligence of a bee, to examine straw after straw until he found the object of his search.

⚡ Just a little theory and calculation would have saved him ninety percent of his labor.

# Thought

⚡ Every effort under duress requires the sacrifice of life energy. I have never paid that price. On the contrary, I let my thoughts flourish.

⚡ In a time not distant, it will be possible to flash any image formed in thought on a screen and render it visible at any place desired. The perfection of this means of reading thought will create a revolution for the better in all our social relations.

⚡ I have thrived on my thoughts.

⚡ In years of experimenting I have found that every thought I conceive, every act I perform, is the result of external impressions on my senses.

⚡ It has cost me years of thought to arrive at certain results, by many believed to be unattainable, for which there are now numerous claimants, and the number of these is rapidly increasing, like that of the colonels in the South after the war.

⚡ There are too many distractions in this life for quality of thought, and it's quality of thought, not quantity, that counts.

# Universe

⚡ A single thought may determine the motion of a universe.

⚡ Every living being is an engine geared to the wheelwork of the universe. Though seemingly affected only by its immediate surrounding, the sphere of external influence extends to infinite distance.

⚡ If you only knew the magnificence of the 3, 6 and 9, then you would have the key to the universe.

⚡ If you want to find the secrets of the universe, think in terms of energy, frequency and vibration.

⚡ My brain is only a receiver, in the Universe there is a core from which we obtain knowledge, strength and inspiration. I have not penetrated into the secrets of this core, but I know that it exists.

⚡ To me, the universe is simply a great machine which never came into being and never will end.

# War

⚡ I inherited from my father, an erudite man who labored hard for peace, an ineradicable hatred of war.

⚡ Out of this war, the greatest since the beginning of history, a new world must be born, a world that would justify the sacrifices offered by humanity. This new world must be a world in which there shall be no exploitation of the weak by the strong, of the good by the evil; where there will be no humiliation of the poor by the violence of the rich; where the products of intellect, science and art will serve society for the betterment and beautification of life, and not the individuals for achieving wealth. This new world shall not be a world of the downtrodden and humiliated, but of free men and free nations, equal in dignity and respect for man.

## Waste

⚡ There is more opportunity for invention in the utilization of waste than in the opening up of new resources.

## Will

⚡ A man cannot be saved from his own foolishness or vice by someone else's efforts or protests, but only by the use of his own will.

## Wireless transmission

⚡ Power can be, and at no distant date will be, transmitted without wires, for all commercial uses, such as the lighting of homes and the driving of aeroplanes. I have discovered the essential principles, and it only remains to develop them commercially. When this is done, you will be able to go anywhere in the world — to the mountain top overlooking your farm, to the arctic, or to the desert — and set up a little equipment that will give you heat to cook with, and light to read by. This equipment will be carried in a satchel not as big as the ordinary suitcase. In years to come wireless lights will be as common on the farms as ordinary electric lights are nowadays in our cities.

⚡ Practical transfer of energy without wires has an extraordinary importance for man.

# Women

⚡ It is not in the shallow physical imitation of men that women will assert first their equality and later their superiority, but in the awakening of the intellect of women.

# Wonders

⚡ We crave for new sensations but soon become indifferent to them. The wonders of yesterday are today common occurrences.

⚡ Speaking of technical achievements, however extraordinary they may be only wonderful to those who have no knowledge of the mechanism or agents linking the effect to the cause.

⚡ That inanimate matter should run into organic forms must be considered a wonder, because we have not yet ascertained why and how this is brought about.

⚡ The human being is one of the greatest mysteries of nature and consequently a wonder. And so is life in all its manifestations. But a time may come when all the subtle and involved processes that are part of our living existence will be laid bare and understood, and then the element of wonder will be removed.

# Work

⚡ Man was born to work, suffer and struggle, and if he doesn't he'll go under.

⚡ Each day we go to our work in the hope of discovering — in the hope that someone, no matter who, may find a solution of one of the pending great problems — and each succeeding day we return to our task with renewed ardor; and even if we are unsuccessful, our work has not been in vain, for in these strivings, in these efforts, we have found hours of untold pleasure, and we have directed our energies to the benefit of mankind.

⚡ I am credited with being one of the hardest workers and perhaps I am, if thought is the equivalent of labour, for I have devoted to it almost all of my waking hours. But if work is interpreted to be a definite performance in a specified time according to a rigid rule, then I may be the worst of idlers.

⚡ I had a veritable mania for finishing whatever I began.

⚡ I strongly believe in the rule of compensation. True awards are always in proportion with work and sacrifices.

⚡ If I try to continue a broken line of thought, I feel a veritable spiritual nausea, then, almost by chance, I go over to another job, surprised by the freshness of mind and ease with which I overcome obstacles which had tormented me before. And as a rule I find answers to difficult questions with the least possible effort.

⚡ Let one concentrate all his energies in one single great effort, let him perceive a single truth, even though he be consumed by the sacred fire, then millions of less gifted men can easily follow. Therefore, it is not as much quantity as quality of work which determines the magnitude of the progress.

⚡ The last 29 days of the month are the toughest.

⚡ There were many days when [I] did not know where my next meal was coming from. But I was never afraid to work, I went where some men were digging a ditch ... [and] said I wanted to work. The boss looked at my good clothes and white hands and laughed to the others ... but he said, "All right. Spit on your hands. Get in the ditch." And I worked harder than anybody. At the end of the day I had $2.

⚡ Three possible solutions of the great problem of increasing human energy are answered by the three words: food, peace, work… Food to increase the mass, peace to diminish the retarding force, and work to increase the force accelerating human movement.

# Photos

# Slike

Nikola Tesla with Rudjer Boscovich
'Theoria Philosophiae Naturalis', New York.

Nikola Tesla sa knjigom Rudjera Boškovića
'Theoria Philosophiae Naturalis', Njujork.

Nikola Tesla with a prototype fluorescent light bulb.

Nikola Tesla sa prototipom fluorescentne lampe.

Nikola Tesla's Polyphase 500 HP AC generator at
the 1893 World Columbian Exposition in Chicago.

Teslin polufazni generator od 500 KS na
Svetskoj kolumbijskoj izložbi 1893. u čikagu.

Nikola Tesla's laboratory in Colorado Springs.

Laboratorija Nikole Tesle u Kolorado Springsu.

Nikola Tesla (1856-1943) at age 34.

Nikola Tesla (1856-1943) u 34. godini.

Nikola Tesla (1856-1943) at age 40.

Nikola Tesla (1856-1943) u 34. godini.

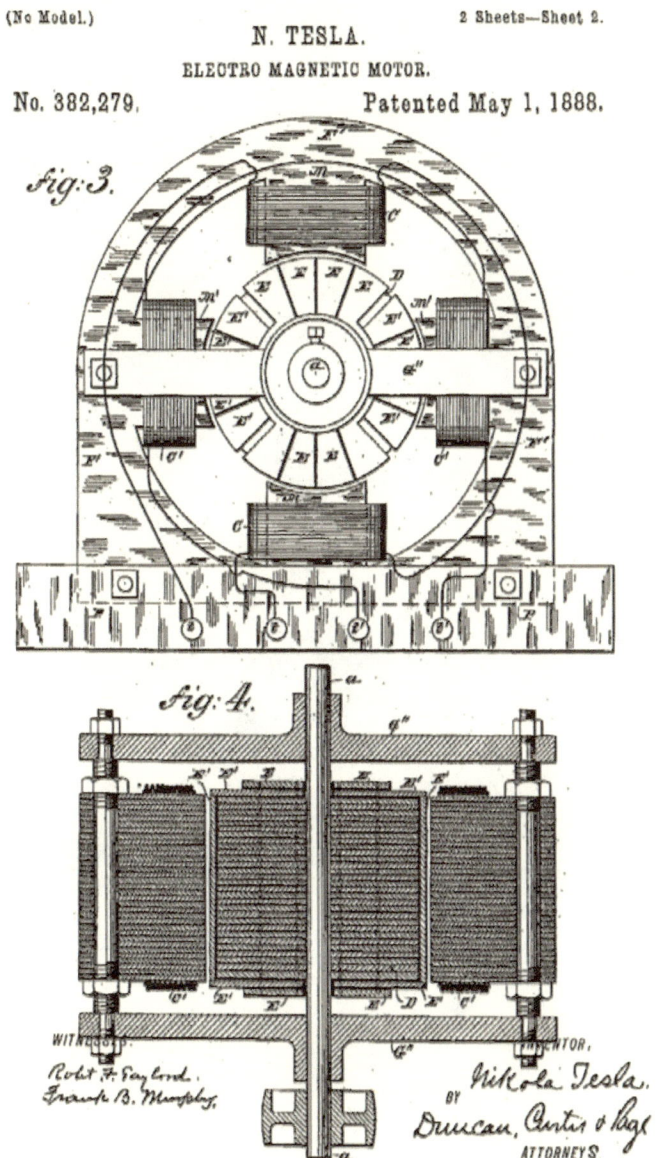

N. TESLA.
ELECTRO MAGNETIC MOTOR.

No. 382,279.                          Patented May 1, 1888.

Nikola Tesla's electro magnetic motor. Patented May 1, 1888.

Teslin elektro magnetski motor patentiran 1. maja 1888.

N. TESLA.
ALTERNATING MOTOR.

No. 555,190.                    Patented Feb. 25, 1896.

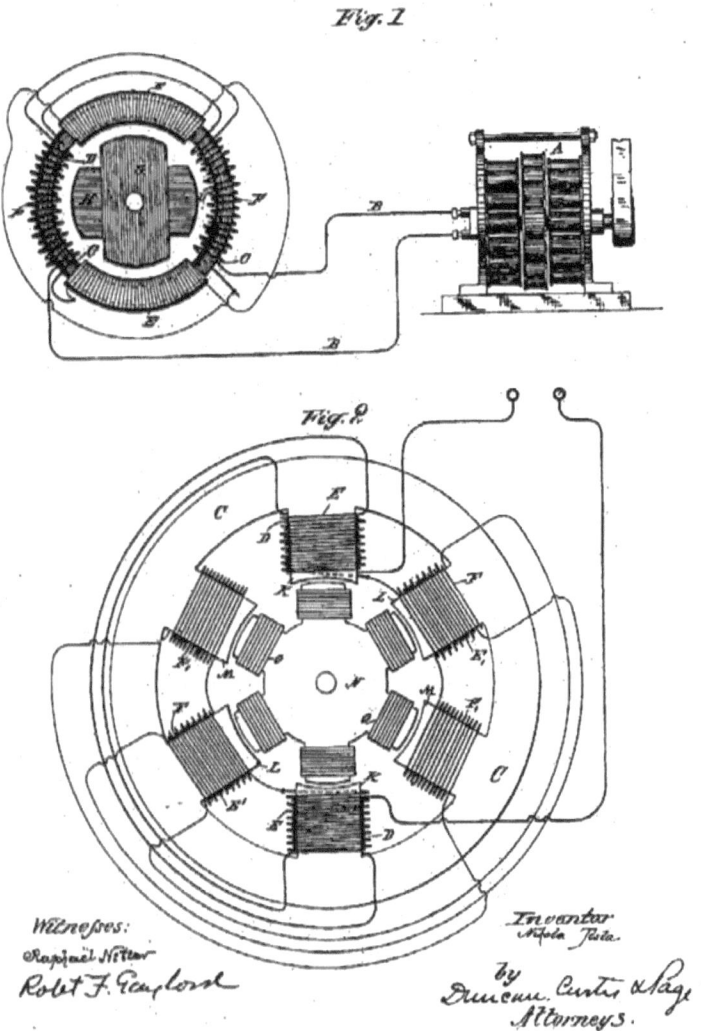

Nikola Tesla's alternating motor. Patented February 25, 1896.

Teslin naizmenični električni motor, patentiran 25. februara 1896.

# Tako je govorio Tesla

Mudrosti jednog od najvećih svetskih pronalazača

Posvećeno svima koji veruju da znanje, u kombinaciji sa inspiracijom i napornim radom, može učiniti ovaj svet mnogo boljim.

Izgleda da sam uvek bio ispred svog vremena.

*Nikola Tesla*

# Nikola Tesla

## Kratka biografija

**Nikola Tesla** se smatra za jednog od najvećih svetskih pronalazača. Elektro inženjer, mašinski inženjer, fizičar i futurista, Tesla je najpoznatiji po izumu naizmenične struje (AC) i sistemu za prenos električne energije. Mnogi su ga smatrali za genija koji je obasjao i elektrificirao svet, moderni Prometeus, jedan od najvećih naučnika u novijoj istoriji. Pravi visionar čiji pronalasci žive i danas.

Tesla je rođen 10. jula 1856. godine u selu Smiljan, blizu Gospića, malom gradiću u tadasnjoj Austro-Ugarskoj carevini. Teslin otac, Milutin, bio je sveštenik srpske pravoslavne crkve, a i njegova majka Georgina (Djuka), rođena Mandić, potiče iz porodice gde je i njen otac bio srpski pravoslavni sveštenik.

Tesla je pohađao osnovnu školu u Smiljanu, nižu gimnaziju u Gospiću, i srednju školu u Karlovcu. Ideja o pravljenju motora naizmenične struje, bez komutatora i četkica, prvi put se javila Tesli 1877 tokom njegove druge godine u studija na politehničkoj školi u Gracu. Tada je profesor Poeschl demonstrirao dinamo koji radi kao motor. Primetivši varnice koje izlaze iz dinama, Tesla je verovao da je moguće stvoriti dinamo koji ne gubi toliko energije ako se koristi naizmenična struja. Iako je bio ismejan zbog ove smešne ideje, Tesla je postao opsednut idejom da bi to moglo da se napravi. Profesor Poesl je bio upoznat sa Teslinim genijem i primetio je da je "sposobnost Nikole u matematici fenomenalna. On zna odgovor na problem još dok ga profesor postavlja na tablu. On nalazi rešenje u svojoj glavi bez da skoro ikada zapiše problem" [https://teslaresearch.jimdo.com/biography-1856-1943/].

Godine 1880 Tesla odlazi u Prag da studira na Karlovom univerzitetu. Međutim, ubrzo napušta Prag i 1881. godine započinje rad kao električar u telefonskoj kompaniji u Budimpešti. Ovde je došao do ideje za indukcioni motor. Putuje u Pariz, nadajući se da će prodati svoju ideju kompaniji Continental Edison, ali oni nisu bili zainteresovani za naizmeničnu struju. Međutim, on je uporno nastavio i 1883. godine završava svoj prvi indukcioni motor. Odlučio je da isproba svoju sreću u Americi ponovo sa Edisonom, nadajući se da će klima biti pogodnija za prihvatanje naizmenične struje (DC).

Sa svojih 28 godina, Nikola Tesla stiže u Njujork sa četiri centa u džepu, sa nekoliko matematičkh proračuna, nacrtom ideje za leteću mašinu, i pisanom preporukom od Charles Batchelor, jednog od Edisonovih poslovnih saradnika u Evropi. Srpski imigrant je bio šokiran onim što je video.

"Ono što sam ostavio bilo je prelepo, umetnički i fascinantno u svakom pogledu; ono što sam video ovde je bilo mehaničko, grubo i neprivlačno. To je [Amerika] vek iza Evrope u civilizaciji." Edison je osetio da ima nešto posebno u Tesli i unajmljuje ga odmah da poboljša neka od njegovih postojenja koja su koristila jednosmernu struju.

Međutim, nakon što je Edison povukao svoju ponudu i obećanje Tesli da će mu dati $50,000 ako reši određeni broj inžinjerijskih problema za Edisonovu kompaniju, tvrdeći da je ponuda ustvari bila šala, Tesla napušta kompaniju i kao besposlen kopa kanale čitavih godinu dana. Nakon toga on formira svoju Tesla kompaniju (Tesla Electric Company) i prima uplate i honorare nakon što je Westinghouse napravio aranžmane za licenciranje tehnologije za njegov AC indukcioni motor.

Tesla je bio radoholičar, radeći često i po 18 sati. Čak i u starosti, Tesla je spavao samo dva ili tri sata noću. On je bio je poznat ne samo zbog svojih naučnih i inženjerijskih dostignuća, već i zbog svojih ličnih navika, rituala, i verovanja. Jedna od njih bila je njegova opsesija sa brojevima, posebno brojevima 3, 6 i 9. On je rekao, "Ako bi samo znali veličanstvenost brojeva 3, 6 i 9, imali biste ključ univerzuma".

Svojim pronalascima Tesla je verovatno doprineo više nego bilo koji drugi naučnik širom sveta. Izmislio je naizmeničnu struju koja se danas koristi, i način na koji se elektricna energija može stvarati i prenositi. U svojoj laboratoriji je koristio fluorescentne sijalice 40 godina pre nego što su one zapravo 'pronadjene'. Tesla je izmislio radio, a ne Marconi koji je ustvari dobio Nobelovu nagradu za ovaj pronalazak. Pokazao je "teleautomaton" uređaj, robotski brod koji se kontroliše radio-talasima. Njegov pronalazak indukcionog motora bio je neverovatno uticajan i još uvek se koristi u aparatima u domaćinstvu, kao što su usisivači, ventilatori, kao i u mnogim drugim industrijskim elektrićnim alatima.

Tesla je prijavio najmanje 308 patenata u 27 zemalja na pet kontinenata. Većina njih — 116 — registrovana je u Americi. 126 su osnovni patenti za prvi put registrovane pronalaske, dok su ostali ekvivalentni patenti, isti pronalazak registrovan u različitim zemljama radi zaštite. Tokom svoje bogate naučne karijere, Tesla je otkrio, dizajnirao i razvio ideje za veći broj važnih izuma — od kojih je većina bila zvanično patentirana od strane drugih pronalazača.

Tesla je bio tehnički i vizionarski genije. Ušao je duboko u tajne prirode i omogućio nam da ih koristimo putem njegovih izuma.

Nikola Tesla je umro u samoći, 7. januara 1943. godine, u svojoj 86-toj godini života, u Njujorku, gde je živeo skoro 60 godina.

# Tesline mudrosti od A do Ž

# Avioni

⚡ Ne oklevam da ovde iznesem kao referencu za budućnost i test tačnosti mojeg naučnog predvidjanja da će leteće mašine i brodovi pokretani bežičnom električnom energijom prestati da budu čudo za desetak godina od danas. Rekao bih možda i za pet godina da ne postoji 'inercija ljudskog razmišljanja' koja se suprotstavlja revolucionarnim idejama.

# Arhimed

⚡ Arhimed je bio moj idol.

# Bežični prenos

⚡ Energija se može, a u ne tako dalekoj budućnosti i biće prenošena bežično, za sve komercijalne svrhe, kao što je osvetljenje kuća i vožnja aviona. Otkrio sam suštinske principe i ostaje samo da ih komercijalno razvijem. Kada se to uradi, moći ćete da odete bilo gde u svetu — do planinskog vrha iznad vaše farme, do Arktika ili do pustinje — i postavite malu opremu koja će vam dati toplinu da kuvate i osvetljenje za čitanje. Ova oprema će se nositi u torbi koja nije veća od obične torbice. U godinama koje dolaze bežične sijalice će biti jednako uobičajene na farmama kao što su obične električne sijalice danas u našim gradovima.

⚡ Praktičan prenos energije bez žica ima izuzetan značaj za čoveka.

# Biseri

⚡ Prizor bisera bi skoro izazvao fit kod mene, ali bio sam fasciniran blistanjem kristala ili predmeta sa oštrim ivicama i ravnim površinama.

# Borba

⚡ Sve što je bilo veliko u prošlosti je bilo ismejano, osuđeno, osporeno, suzbijano — da bi se nakon trijumfalne borbe pojavilo još snažnije.

# Bog

⚡ Dar duhovne moći dolazi od Boga, Božanskog Bića, i ako usredsredimo naše umove na tu istinu, postajemo uskladjeni s tom velikom moći.

⚡ Hrišćanstvo i nauka nas inspirišu da radimo sto bolje možemo kako bi povećali učinak ljudskog roda.

⚡ Ono što jedan čovek zove Bog, drugi naziva zakonima fizike.

# Breskva

⚡ Dobijem groznicu pogledavši u breskvu.

# Budućnost

⚡ Neka budućnost kaže istinu i oceni svakog prema njegovom radu i dostignućima. Sadašnjost je njihova, budućnost, za koju sam stvarno radio, je moja.

⚡ Otkriće nove naučne istine biće važnije od prepirke diplomata.

⚡ Pojedincu neće biti dopušteno da postigne veliko bogatstvo i moć; njegova će privatnost biti ugrožena na hiljadu načina. On će biti ograničen u svojim naporima u svakom smeru — praktično će nestati u talasu kolektivizma koji će potopiti svet.

⚡ Ova materijalistička plima može se sprečiti samo idealizmom, koji je sila koja nastoji osloboditi ono što nazivamo čovekovom dušom od fizičkih okova. Ali, iako bi mogli postojati periodi u kojima će se smenjivati ova dva načela — materijaliazm i idealizam — konačno će nadvladati materijalističke tendencije.

⚡ Danas najcivilizovanije zemlje sveta troše najveći deo svojih prihoda na rat, a najmanje na obrazovanje. Dvadeset i prvi vek će preokrenuti taj poredak.

⚡ Budućnost će pokazati da li će moja sadašnja predvidjanja biti toliko tačna kao što su bila do sada.

# Cilj

⚡ Nemojte ciljati na ono u šta gledate, već na ono što nameravate pogoditi.

# Civilizacija

⚡ Širenje civilizacije može se uporediti sa vatrom; prvo, slaba iskra, posle trepćući plamen, a zatim snažan plamen koji stalno povećava brzinu i moć.

# Čitanje

⚡ Kad god sam uspeo, pokušao sam da zadovoljim svoju strast za čitanjem.

# Čovek

⚡ Vidim prijatelja u bolu, isto zaboli i mene: moj prijatelj i ja smo jedno ... svi smo jedno.

⚡ Ja sam bio samo automat kome je podarena mogućnost kretanja, koji reaguje na stimulanse organa čula, i koji u skladu sa tim razmišlja i postupa.

⚡ Čovek, kao i univerzum, je mašina.

⚡ Pojedinac je prolazan, rase i narodi dolaze i odlaze, ali čovek ostaje. U tome je velika razlika između pojedinca i celine.

⚡ Svesno prouzrokovati rođenje i smrt materije bilo bi čovekovo najveće delo, to bi mu dalo moć fizičkog stvaralanja i ostvarenje svoje krajnje sudbine.

# Čovečanstvo

⚡ Želja koja me vodi u sve što radim jeste želja da se sile prirode iskoriste za dobrobit čovečanstva.

⚡ Ima nešto u meni što bi moglo biti iluzija, kao što je to često slučaj s mladim oduševljenim ljudima, ali ako bih imao sreću da postignem neke od mojih ideala, bilo bi to u ime čitavog čovječanstva.

⚡ Napredak i razvoj čoveka su od neizmerne važnosti za čovečanstvo i u suštini zavise od inovacija.

# Čuda

⚡ Žudimo za novim senzacijama, ali ubrzo postajemo ravnodušni prema njima. Jučerašnja čuda danas su uobičajene pojave.

⚡ Govoreći o tehničkim dostignućima, koliko god bila izvanredna ona mogu biti samo divna onima koji nemaju saznanja o mehanizmu ili faktorima koji povezuju efekat sa uzrokom.

⚡ Da nežive materije treba da prelaze u organske forme, mora se smatrati čudom, zato što još nismo utvrdili zašto i kako do toga dolazi. Ljudsko biće je jedna od najvećih misterija prirode i stoga čudo. Isto je i sa životom u svim njegovim manifestacijama. Ali možda će doći vreme kada će svi suptilni i uključeni procesi koji su deo našeg živog postojanja biti otkriveni i shvaćeni. Tada će element čuda biti uklonjen.

# Čula

⚡ Naša čula nam omogućavaju da sagledamo samo manje delove spoljnjeg sveta. Naša rasprava se odvija na maloj udaljenosti. Naš pogled je ometan zidom i senkom. Da bismo se upoznali jedan s drugim, moramo zaobići sferu našeg osećaja percepcije.

# Detinjstvo

⚡ Još od detinjstva bio sam predodredjen za sveštenstvo. Ova perspektiva se nadvila nada mnom kao kakav mračan oblak.

# Disrupcija

⚡ To je radikalna promena u smislu da bi njen uspeh značio napuštanje zastarelih vrsta bazičnih pokretača na koje su potrošene milijarde dolara.

# Dokolica

⚡ Isuvise dokolice vodi civilizaciju u propast.

# Duša

⚡ Tokom vekova razvijeni su mehanizmi beskonačno složeni, ali ono što nazivamo 'dušom' ili 'duhom' nije ništa drugo do suma funkcionisanja tela. Kada ovo funkcionisanje prestane, "duša" ili "duh" prestanu na isti način.

# Elektricitet

⚡ Kao i u prirodi, sve je oseka i plima, sve je kretanje talasa, tako da se čini da će na sve grane industrije, naizmenična struja — kretanje električnih talasa — imati svoj uticaj.

⚡ Dan kada tačno saznamo šta je "elektricitet", bićemo svedoci događaja verovatno većeg i važnijeg od bilo kojeg drugog zabeleženog u istoriji ljudske rase. Doći će vreme kada će udobnost a možda i samo postojanje čoveka zavisiti od tog čudesnog otkrića.

⚡ Osećaj neprestano raste u meni da sam bio prvi koji je čuo pozdrav jedne planete drugoj.

⚡ Ova planeta, sa svom svojom ogromnom veličinom, za električnu struju doslovno ne predstavlja ništa više nego jednu malu metalnu kuglu.

⚡ Oko jednostavnog gvozdenog prstena namotamo žicu; povežemo je sa generatorom, i sa čuđenjem i radošću posmatramo dejstvo čudnih sila koje smo uveli u igru, što nam omogućava željenu transformaciju, prenos i usmeravanje energije.

⚡ Sada vam moram reći o čudnom iskustvu koje se odrazilo na moj kasniji život. Imali smo jedan hladan period sa sušom kakva ranije nije primećena. Ljudi koji su išli po snegu ostavljali su svjetleći trag. Kao kad bih pomilovao leđa mački, snop svjetlosti bi došao, a moja ruka bi proizvela kišu iskri. Otac je prokomentarisao da to nije ništa drugo nego elektricitet, isto što i vi vidite na stablima u oluji. Moja majka je izgledala uznemirena. Prestani da se igraš sa mačkom, rekla je, mogao bi izazvati požar. Razmišljao sam apstraktno. Da li je priroda mačka? Ako je tako, ko njoj mazi leđa? To može biti samo Bog, zaključio sam. Ne mogu preterati učinak tog divnog pogleda na moju dečiju maštu. Iz dana u dan sam se pitao što je elektricitet i nisam našao odgovor. Od tada je prošlo osamdeset godina i još uvijek postavljam isto pitanje, a odgovora nemam.

# Električna energija

⚡ Ali među svim ovim mnogim oblastima istraživanja, brojnim industrijskim granama, novim i starim, koje se brzo proširuju, postoji jedna oblast koja je važnija za svih drugih — ona je od najvećeg značaja za udobnost i blagostanje, da ne kazem i za postojanje čovečanstva, a to je oblast prenosa električne energije.

⚡ Elekrična energija je prisutna svuda i u neograničenim količinama. Ona može da pokrene sve mašine sveta bez potrebe za ugljem, naftom, ili gasom.

# Elektrotehnika

⚡ Elektrotehnika nam je otkrila intimniji odnos između različitih sila i fenomena i na taj način nas dovela do potpunijeg razumevanja prirode i njenih mnogih manifestacija za naša čula.

⚡ Elektrotehnika nam je otkrila pravu prirodu svetlosti, pružila nam nebrojene uređaje i precizne instrumente, i time je dosta dodala tačnosti našeg znanja.

⚡ Od različitih grana elektro istraživanja, možda najinteresantnija i koja najviše obećava je ona koja se bavi naizmeničnim strujama.

⚡ Tako iznenađujuće su činjenice u vezi s tim, da bi izgledalo kao da je i sam Tvorac stvorio ovu planetu koristeći elektrotehniku.

# Energija

⚡ Nema energije u materiji osim one koja je dobijena iz okoline.

⚡ Apsolutno je nemoguće pretvoriti masu u energiju.

⚡ Okrećemo se beskrajnim prostorom, s nezamislivom brzinom, sve oko nas se vrti, sve se kreće, sve je energija. Mora da postoji neki direktniji način korišćenja ove energije. Zatim, uz svjetlost dobijenu iz medija, sa snagom izvedenom iz nje, sa svim oblicima energije dobijenim bez napora, iz neiscrpnog izvora, čovečanstvo će napredovati s divovskim koracima. I samo razmišljanje o tim veličanstvenim mogućnostima proširuje naše umove, jača naše nade i ispunjava naša srca vrhunskim zadovoljstvom.

⚡ Energija je svuda u prostoru. Da li je ova energija statična ili kinetička! Ako su statičke naše nade su uzaludne; ako je kinetička — a znamo da je sigurno ta — onda je to samo pitanje vremena kada će ljudi uspeti da priključe svoje mašine direktno na sam zamajac prirode.

⚡ Ali mi se nećemo zadovoljiti poboljšanjem parnih i eksplozivnih motora ili izumom novih baterija; imamo nešto mnogo bolje na čemu treba da radimo, da ispunimo veći zadatak. Moramo razviti sredstva za dobijanje energije iz izvora koje su trajno neiscrpni, da usavršimo metode koje ne podrazumevaju potrošnju i otpad bilo kojeg materijala.

# Frekvencija

⚡ Sve stvari imaju frekvenciju i vibraciju.

# Golubovi

⚡ Hranim golubove, hiljade njih već godinama. Ali, bila je jedna prelepa ptica čisto bela sa svetlo sivim vrhovima krila; ona je bila drugačija. Bila je to ženka. Mogao sam samo da poželim i da je nazovem i ona bi doletela do mene. Voleo sam tu golubicu kao što muškarac voli ženu a i ona je volela mene. Sve dok sam je imao, moj život je imao svrhu.

# Hrana

⚡ Nema sumnje da je neka biljna hrana, kao što je ovsena kaša, ekonomičnija od mesa, i superiornija za naš fizički i umni rad. Šta više, takva hrana definitivno manje opterećuje naše organe za varenje, čineći nas zadovoljnijim i društvenijim, stvarajući pri tome opšte dobro od neprocenjive vrednosti.

# Hidroenergija

⚡ Imamo mnogo spomenika prošlih perioda; imamo palate i piramide, grčke hramove i hrišćanske katedrale. U njima je prikazana moć ljudi, veličina naroda, ljubav prema umetnosti i verska odanost. Ali spomenik na Niagari ima nešto svoje, više u skladu s našim sadašnjim mislima i tendencijama. To je spomenik vredan našeg naučnog doba, pravi spomenik prosvetljenja i mira. On označava stavljanje prirodnih sila u službu čoveku, prestanak barbarskih metoda, olakšanje od želje i patnje za milione.

# Ideali

⚡ Borba za egzistenciju je smanjena, razvoj bi trebalo da bude vodjen idealima a ne materijalnim ciljevima.

⚡ Moramo svi imati neki ideal koji će upravljati našim ponašanjem i zadovoljiti nas, ali ne materijalno. To može biti religija, umetnost, nauka, bilo šta, samo je važno da deluje kao ne-materijalna sila.

# Ideja

⚡ O novoj ideji se ne sme suditi na osnovu trenutnih rezultata.

⚡ Budite sami, to je tajna pronalazaka; biti sam, to je kada se radjaju ideje.

⚡ Ne brine me što su ukrali moju ideju... Brine me da nemaju svoje.

⚡ Nove ideje se postepeno usvajaju. Neizbežno je da će oni koji su na čelu napretka zadržati svoja mesta. Naš je život sada toliko regulisan da nikakav napredak ne može potpuno narušiti postojeći poredak.

⚡ Sprovođenje u praksu sirove ideje, kao što se generalno radi, smatram za gubljenje energije, novca i vremena.

⚡ Praktični uspeh ideje, bez obzira na inherentne mogućnosti, zavisi od stava savremenika.

⚡ Kada dobijem ideju, odmah počinjem da je gradim u svojoj mašti. Menjam konstrukciju, pravim poboljšanja i upravljam uređajem u mislima. Apsolutno mi nije bitno da li upravljam turbinom u mislima ili je testiram u svojoj radionici.

⚡ Sa idejama je kao sa vrtoglavom visinom na koju se penjete: Na početku ona izaziva nelagodnost i želite da se spustite, neverujući u sopstvene moći; ali ubrzo, daljina životnih previranja i inspirativan uticaj nadmorske visine smiruju vašu krv; vaš korak postaje čvrst i siguran i počinjete da tražite jos vrtoglavije visine.

## Imaginacija

⚡ Naša prva nastojanja isključivo su instinktivni podsticaj živahne mašte i ne-discipline.

⚡ Kada dobijem ideju, odmah počinjem da je gradim u svojoj mašti. Menjam konstrukciju, pravim poboljšanja i upravljam uređajem u mislima. Apsolutno mi nije bitno da li upravljam turbinom u mislima ili je testiram u svojoj radionici.

## Instinkt

⚡ Instinkt je nešto što prevazilazi znanje. Imamo, nesumnjivo, izvesna finija vlakna koja nam omogućavaju da sagledamo istine kada je logično zaključivanje, ili bilo koji drugi svesni napor mozga, besmislen.

⚡ Naši prvi napori su čisto instiktivni potezi živopisne i nedisciplinovane mašte. Kako starimo, razum postaje sve jači, sve više sistematski i planski. Ali ti rani impulsi, mada ne odmah produktivni, su od najvećeg značaja i mogu oblikovati naše sudbine. Zaista, sada osećam da sam ih tada shvatio i kultivisao, umesto što sam ih potisnuo, dodao bih značajnu vrednost mom doprinosu ovom svetu.

# Inteligencija

⚡ Moja uverenost je postala tako snažna da više ne gledam na ovaj plan prenosa energije i inteligencije kao puku teorijsku mogućnost, već kao ozbiljan problem elektrotehničkog inženjeringa, koji se mora jednog dana mora izvesti.

# Introspekcija

⚡ Cenite neprocenjivu vrednost introspekcije u očuvanju života.

⚡ Izbegavanje imaginacije i ignorisanje stvarnih opasnosti je česta greška.

⚡ Ništa ne ulazi u naše umove ili određuje naše postupke što nije direktno ili indirektno odgovor na stimulacije koji preplavljuju naše čulne organe iznutra.

⚡ Većina ljudi je toliko zanesena kontemplacijom spoljnjeg sveta da su potpuno nesvesni onoga što se dešava unutar njih.

# Jezik

⚡ Osećao sam da je vreme koje sam proveo učeći jezike, književnost i umetnost izgubljeno; ali kasnije, naravno, saznao sam da to nije tako.

⚡ Naučio sam desetak jezika, proučavao literaturu i umetnost, proveo svoje najbolje godine u bibliotekama čitajući sve što mi je došlo pod ruku, i mada sam ponekad osjećao da gubim vreme, brzo sam shvatio da je to bila najbolja stvar koju sam ikad učinio.

⚡ Međusobno razumevanje biće beskonačno lakše pomoću jednog univerzalnog jezika.

# Lenjost

⚡ Ja ne verujem u lenjost i voleo bih da vidim da su besposličari izbrisani sa lica zemlje; ali želim da oni koji su voljni da rade ostvare svoje rezultate sa najmanje uloženog truda i na najbolji način.

# Ljubav

⚡ Nije stvar u ljubavi koju dobijate, već u ljubavi koju dajete.

# Ljudi

⚡ Svi smo mi jedno. Ljudi su međusobno povezani nevidljivim silama. Iako imamo slobodu misli i delovanja, držimo se zajedno, kao zvezde na nebeskom svodu, s neraskidivim vezama. Te se veze ne mogu videti, ali ih možemo osetiti.

⚡ Svako bi trebalo da smatra svoje telo kao neprocenjiv dar od onoga koga voli iznad svega, čudesno umetničko delo neopisive lepote, čudo izvan ljudskog shvatanja, a tako nežno da ga reč, dah, pogled, odbijanje, misao može povrediti.

⚡ Naša čula omogućuju nam da vidimo samo manji deo spoljnjeg sveta.

⚡ Naše vrline i naši nedostaci su nerazdvojivi, kao sila i materija. Kada se odvoje, nema više čoveka.

⚡ Ljudsko biće je samohodni automat koji je potpuno pod kontrolom spoljnih uticaja. Mada izgledaju voljni i unaprijed određeni, njegovi postupci nisu vodjeni iznutra, nego spolja. On je kao splav koga valovi uzburkanog mora bacaju okolo.

⚡ Iako slobodni da mislimo i radimo, držimo se zajedno, poput zvezda na nebu, nerazdvojivo povezani. Te se veze ne mogu videti, ali ih možemo osetiti.

# Kamfor

⚡ Ako se i komadić kamfora nalazio bilo gde u kući izazvao bi mi najgore nelagodnosti.

# Karijera

⚡ Po ironiji sudbine, moje prvo zaposlenje je bilo kao tehnicki crtač. Mrzeo sam crtež; za mene je to bila najgora muka. Na sreću, to nije bilo dugo pre nego sto sam obezbedio sebi poziciju koju sam tražio, glavni električar u telefonskoj kompaniji.

# Knjige

⚡ Od svega najviše sam voleo knjige.

⚡ Jednom prilikom sam počeo da citam dela Voltera, kada sam shvatio, na moje zaprepašćenje, da ima blizu sto velikih tomova štampanih sitnim slovima koje je to čudovište napisalo dok je pio sedamdeset dve čaše crne kafe dnevno. Morao sam da to završim, ali kada sam završio i poslednju knjigu bio sam sretan, i rekao sam 'Nikad više!'

# Kockanje

⚡ Bio sam jednako ravnodušan prema bilo kom obliku kockanja kao i prema čačkanju zuba.

# Kosa

⚡ Ne bih dodirnuo kosu drugih ljudi osim, možda, uz pretnju revolvera.

# Kristali

⚡ Kristali su živa bića sa početka stvaranja sveta.

⚡ U kristalu imamo čist dokaz postojanja principa stvaranja života, i mada uprkos svega nemožemo da razumemo život kristala — on je ipak živo biće.

# Majndfulnes

⚡ Savršena čistoća vazduha, neponovljiva lepota neba, impozantan pogled na visoki planinski venac, tiha i mirna mesta — uvek su bili idealni uslovi za naučno zapažanje.

# Markoni

⚡ Markoni je dobar momak. Pustite ga da nastavi. Koristi sedamnaest mojih patenata.

# Mark Tvejn

⚡ Jednog dana sam dobio nekoliko knjiga nove literature mnogo drugacije od bilo čega što sam ranije pročitao i tako zadivljujuće, da sam zaboravio moje beznadežno stanje. Bila su to ranija dela Mark Tvejna i za njih vezujem moj čudesni oporavak koji je usledio. Dvadeset i pet godina kasnije, kada sam upoznao g. Klemensa i kada smo uspostavili prijateljstvo između nas, rekao sam mu o tom iskustvu. Bio sam zapanjen kada sam video kako je veliki majstor smeha zaplakao.

# Matematika

⚡ Jedva da postoji tema koja se ne može matematički sagledati, efekti izračunati ili rezultati utvrditi unapred koristeći postojeće teorijske i praktične podatke.

# Mentalna moć

⚡ Neprestani mentalni napor razvio je moju moć zapažanja i omogućio mi da otkrijem istinu od velike važnosti.

# Minđuše

⚡ Imao sam strašnu averziju prema ženskim minđušama, ali mi se ostali nakit, kao recimo narukvice, svidjao, u zavisnosti od dizajna.

# Mir

⚡ Mir može doći samo kao prirodna posledica univerzalnog prosvetljenja i spajanja rasa, a još uvijek smo daleko od ove blažene realizacije.

⚡ Ono što sada želimo je bliži kontakt i bolje razumijevanje među pojedincima i zajednicama širom zemlje i eliminaciju egoizma i ponosa koji je uvek sklon da svet uroni u iskonsko varvarstvo i sukobe.

⚡ Najveća vrednost mog izuma će biti rezultat njegovog uticaja na rat I oružje, jer će zbog svoje određene i neograničene destruktivnosti nastojati da stvori i održai trajni mir među narodima.

⚡ Univerzalni mir kao rezultat kumulativnih vekovnih napora može brzo nastati — ne kao kristal koji odjednom stvori rešenje koje se polako pripremalo.

# Moral

⚡ Naučna dostignuća mogu uticati čak i na naš moral i običaje.

# Misao

⚡ Svaki napor pod prisilom zahteva žrtvovanje životne energije. Nikad nisam platio tu cenu. Naprotiv, dopustio sam svojim mislima da cvetaju.

⚡ U vremenu koje nije udaljeno, biće moguće na ekranu bljesnuti bilo koju sliku formiranu u mislima i učiniti je vidljivom na bilo kojem željenom mjestu. Savršenstvo ovog načina čitanja misli će stvoriti revoluciju na bolje u svim našim društvenim odnosima.

⚡ Sopstvene misli su mi bile nadahnuce.

⚡ U godinama eksperimentisanja otkrio sam da je svaka misao koju zamislim, sve što uradim, rezultat spoljašnjih utisaka na moja čula.

⚡ Koštalo me više godina razmišljanja da dođem do određenih rezultata, koje su mnogi smatrali nedostižnim, za koje sada postoje brojni pretendenti, a njihov broj se ubrzano povećava kao broj pukovnika na jugu nakon rata.

⚡ Previše je ometanja u ovom životu da bi se postigao kvalitet misli, a kvalitet, ne kvantitet, je taj koji se računa.

# Mržnja

⚡ Ako bi se mržnja mogla pretvoriti u električnu energiju, osvetlila bi čitav svet.

# Muzika

⚡ Ja sam deo svetlosti, a to je muzika. Čestice svetlosti su pisane beleške. Munja može biti čitava sonata. Hiljadu munja je koncert.

# Nagrade

⚡ Uzdržavanje nije uvek bilo u skladu sa mojim ukusom, ali moja prijatna iskustva su ogromna nagrada.

⚡ Prave nagrade su uvek proporcionalne radu i žrtvovanju.

# Napredak

⚡ Ljudska aktivnost je postala tako rasprostranjena i intenzivna da se godine računaju kao vekovi napretka. Nema više preznojenja u mraku ili slučajnog otkrića. Rezultati prate jedni druge kao karike na lancu. Takva je snaga akumuliranog znanja i uvid u prirodne zakone i pojave da se budući događaji postaju jasni deo naše vizije.

# Natprirodan

⚡ Na dan kada nauka počne da proučava ne-fizičke pojave, ona će učiniti veći napredak u jednoj deceniji nego u svim prethodnim vekovima svog postojanja.

# Naučnik

⚡ Čovečanstvo još nije dovoljno napredovalo da se dobrovoljno prepusti osećajima nekog pronalazača.

⚡ Čovek od nauke ne teži neposrednom rezultatu. On ne očekuje da će njegove napredne ideje biti lako prihvaćene. Njegov rad je poput onog ko seje za budućnost. Njegova dužnost je da postavi temelje za one koji dolaze, i ukaže im na put. On živi, trudi se i nada se.

⚡ Naučnici danas razmišljaju duboko umesto jasno. Neko mora biti zdrav da misli jasno, ali neko može razmišljati i duboko a biti sasvim lud.

⚡ Današnji naučnici su zamenili matematiku sa eksperimentima, i lutaju od jednačine do jednačine da bi na kraju stvorili strukturu koja nema veze sa stvarnošću.

⚡ Imao sam samo malo vremena da posvetim ispunjavanju obaveze koja je, pored one da se najveći napori usmere na vredna istraživanja u izabranim oblastima, najvažniji za naučnog radnika; naime, pružanju tačnih zapisa dobijenih rezultata

# Nauka

⚡ Nauka i pronalasci imaju toliku moć da će dovesti do sopstvenog kraja.

⚡ Nauka je lična perverzija osim ako je njen krajnji cilj dobrobit čovečanstva.

⚡ Nauka se suprotstavlja teološkim dogmama jer se nauka zasniva na činjenicama.

⚡ Ako se dve planete sudare u određeno vreme i na određenom mestu, to je studentu pozitivne nauke neizbežan rezultat prethodnih interakcija između tela; i ako bi naše znanje bilo adekvatno, mogli bismo precizno predvideti taj događaj.

# Neznanje

⚡ Manjkava observacija je samo oblik neznanja i odgovorna je za mnoge morbidne pojmove i prevladavajuće glupe ideje.

⚡ Paradoksalno je, ali istinito, reći, da što više znamo, u apsolutnom smislu naše neznanje je sve veće, jer samo kroz prosvećenje postajemo svesni naših ograničenja. Upravo jedan od najdragocenijih rezultata intelektualnog razvoja je kontinuirano otvaranje novih i većih perspektiva.

⚡ Biće slavnije boriti se protiv neznanja nego umirati na bojnom polju.

⚡ Od svih otpora, onaj koji najviše retardira ljudski napredak je neznanje, što je Buda nazvao "najveće zlo na svetu". Trenje koji je rezultat neznanja može se smanjiti samo širenjem znanja i ujedinjenjem heterogenih elemenata čovečanstva. Nema većeg razloga da se uloži napor.

# Nesporazumi

⚡ Borba između pojedinaca, kao i izmedju vlada i nacija, neizbežno je rezultat nesporazuma u najširem tumačenju ovog termina. Nesporazumi su uvek uzrokovani nesposobnošću da se poštuju razlike u gledištu onog drugog.

# Novac

⚡ Novac ne predstavlja takvu vrednost kao što su mu ljudi dali. Sav moj novac je uložen u eksperimente sa kojim sam napravio nova otkrića koja omogućavaju ljudskom rodu malo lakši život.

⚡ Nijedna želja za materijalnim prednostima nije mi bila vodilja u mom radu, mada se nadam, u svrhu nastavka rada, da će uskoro doći i to, naravno, kao nadoknada za vredne usluge pružene nauci i industriji.

⚡ Tehnički napredak nas neizbežno dovodi do najgore vrste materijalizma. I neće proci mnogo dugo pre nego što će društveni sistem pčelinjeg života postati univerzalan.

# Novi svet

⚡ Novi svet se mora stvoriti. Svet koji bi opravdavao žrtve koje čovečanstvo cini. Ovaj novi svet mora biti svet u kojem neće biti iskorišćavanja slabih od jačih, dobra od zla, gde neće biti poniženja siromašnih od nasilja bogatih, gde će proizvodi intelekta, nauke i umetnosti služiti društvu za poboljšanje i ulepšanje života, a ne pojedincima za postizanje bogatstva. Ovaj novi svet neće biti svet potlačenih i poniženih, već slobodnih ljudi i slobodnih naroda, podjednako dostojanstvenih i poštovanih.

# Otpad

⚡ Postoji više mogućnosti za pronalaske u oblasti korišćenja otpada nego u otkrivanju novih resursa.

# Osećaji

⚡ Neko može osetiti iznenadni talas tuge i prevrnuti svoj mozak tražeći objašnjenje, da bi primetio da je to prouzrokovano oblakom koji je presekao zrake sunca.

# Patriotizam

⚡ Sve dok postoje različite nacionalnosti, biće patriotizma. Taj osećaj mora biti iskorenjen iz naših srca pre uspostavljanja trajnog mira. To bi trebalo zameniti ljubavlju prema prirodi i naučnom idealu. Nauka i pronalasci su jake snage koje će dovesti do njegovog nestanka.

# Politički savezi

⚡ To su samo novi sistemi za stavljanje slabijih na milost i nemilost jačih.

# Praštanje

⚡ Više puta ste me uvredili, ali ja, kao hrišćanin i filozof, uvek sam vam opraštao i sažaljevao vas zbog vaših grešaka.

# Prilika

⚡ Veliki trenutci rađaju velike prilike.

# Priroda

⚡ Pad jednog zraka svetlosti sa neke daleke zvezde na oko tiranina u prošlosti možda je promenio tok njegovog života, možda je promenio sudbinu nacija, možda je transformisao površinu zemlje, tako su složeni, tako neshvatljivo kompleksni prirodni procesi.

⚡ Dao bih hiljadu tajni prirode na koje sam slučajno naišao, u zamenu za ovu jednu koju sam izvukao iz prirode, uprkos svim čudima i opasnostima s kojima sam se suočio.

⚡ Ako ne znate kako, posmatrajte prirodne pojave, one ce vam dati jasne odgovore i inspiraciju.

⚡ Ni na koji način ne možemo doći na tako neverovatnu ideju o veličini prirode nego kada smatramo da su u skladu sa zakonom o očuvanju energije, do beskonačnosti, sile u savršenoj ravnoteži, a samim tim i da energija jedne misli može odrediti kretanje univerzuma.

⚡ Sasvim je očigledno da ovo rasipanje ne može trajati u nedogled, jer geološka istraživanja dokazuju da su naši izvori goriva ograničeni. Tako je bilo ogromno njegovo crpljenje poslednjih godina da se u daljini nazire mogućnost njegovog totalnog nestanka.

⚡ Istorija nauke pokazuje da su teorije prolazne.

⚡ Uz svaku novu istinu koja se otkrije dolazimo do boljeg razumevanja prirode, a naše koncepcije i stavovi se menjaju.

# Privatnost

⚡ Možda ćemo se uskoro tako naviknuti na ovo stanje stvari da niko neće osetiti ni najmanje stida dok je svestan da su njegov skelet i drugi delovi tela gledani od strane nepristojnih posmatrača.

# Pronalasci

⚡ Mislim da ne postoji nikakvo uzbuđenje koje može proći kroz ljudsko srce poput onog koje pronalazač oseti kad vidi neku tvorevinu svog mozga kako se uspešno ostvaruje... Zbog takvih emocija čovek zaboravi na hranu, spavanje, prijatelje, ljubav, na sve.

⚡ Mislim da ne možete navesti mnoge velike pronalaske koje su napravili venčani ljudi.

⚡ Na moju nesreću stotine pronalazaka nisam mogao da registrujem kao svoje patente.

⚡ Pronalazak je najvažniji proizvod kreativnog mozga čoveka. Krajna svrha je potpuno ovladavanje uma nad materijalnim svetom, korišćenje prirode za ljudske potrebe.

⚡ Moj metod je drugačiji. Ja ne žurim ka stvarnom radu. Kada dobijem novu ideju, odmah počinjem da to gradim u svojoj mašti, napravim poboljšanja i upravljam uređajem u svojoj glavi. Kada sam otišao toliko daleko da uključim sve u moj pronalazak, svako moguće poboljšanje koje mogu da zamislim, a kad ne vidim nikakvu grešku bilo gde, prelazim na konkretizaciju krajnjeg proizvoda mog uma.

⚡ Možda je u ovom sadašnjem svetu bolje da se revolucionarna ideja ili pronalazak na samom početku ometaju i tretiraju loše umesto da se pomažu i podržavaju.

⚡ Progresivni razvoj čoveka životno zavisi od pronalazaka. To je najvažniji proizvod njegovog kreativnog uma.

# Pronalazač

⚡ Divio sam se delima umetnika, ali po mom mišljenju, to su bile samo senke i sličnosti. Pronalazač, mislio sam, daje svetu opipljiva dela koje žive i rade.

⚡ Ako vam se ne dopada dovoljno da prepoznate u meni pronalazača principa, bar me zovite 'pronalazačem nekih lepih komada električnih aparata'.

⚡ Tek sam u mladosti shvatio da sam pronalazač.

⚡ Pronalazači nemaju vremena za bračni život.

⚡ Pronalazač pronalazi ogromnu nadoknadu u zadovoljstvu koje nudi njegovo delo i saznanje da je on pojedinac izvanrednih sposobnosti bez kojih bi naša vrsta ubzo izumrla u žestokoj borbi protiv nemilosrdne prirode.

# Proviđenje

⚡ Vrlo verovatno bi moja karijera bila okončana pre svog vremena da mi Proviđenje nije obezbedilo mehanizam odbrane koji je postajao snažniji iz godine u godinu i koji se nepogrešivo aktivirao kad god su moje snage bile pri kraju.

# Rad

⚡ Čovek je rođen da radi, trpi i bori se, i ako to ne učini propašće.

⚡ Svakog dana idemo na naš posao u nadi da ćemo otkriti — u nadi da će neko, bez obzira na to ko, naći rešenje jednog od velikih problema — i svakog narednog dana vraćamo se našem zadatku s obnovljenim žarom; i čak i ako smo neuspešni, naš rad nije bio uzaludan, jer smo u ovim nastojanjima, u tim naporima, našli sate neispričanog zadovoljstva, i usmerili naše energije u korist čovečanstva.

⚡ Meni se pripisuje da sam jedan od najvećih radnika, a možda i jesam, ako je misao ekvivalent rada, jer sam mu posvetio skoro svo svoje budno vreme. Ali, ako se rad tumači kao definitivan učinak u određenom vremenu prema rigidnom pravilu, onda mogu biti najgori neradnik.

⚡ Imao sam pravu maniju da završim sve što sam započeo.

⚡ Čvrsto verujem u pravilo kompenzacije. Prava nagrada je uvek u srazmeri sa radom i žrtvama.

⚡ Ako pokušam da nastavim prekinutu liniju misli, osetim istinsku duhovnu mučninu, onda, skoro slučajno, pređem na drugi posao, iznenađen svežinom uma i lakoćom kojom prevazilazim prepreke koje su me ranije mučile. Po pravilu, pronalazim odgovore na teška pitanja sa najmanjim naporom.

⚡ Ako neko koncentriše svu svoju energija u jedan jedini veliki napor, neka sagleda jednu istinu, iako je progutan svetom vatrom, onda milioni manje nadarenih ljudi mogu lako da prate. Otuda nije toliko kolicina koliko kvalitet rada koji određuje veličinu napretka.

⚡ Poslednjih 29 dana u mesecu su najteži.

⚡ Bilo je mnogo dana kada nisam znao odakle dolazi moj sledeći obrok. Ali nikada se nisam plašio da radim, otišao sam tamo gde su neki ljudi kopali jarak... rekao sam im da želim da radim. Šef je pogledao moju dobru odjeću i bijele ruke i nasmijao se sa ostalima... ali on je rekao: 'U redu. Pljuni u ruke. Uđi u jarak'. I ja sam radio više od bilo koga. Na kraju dana sam imao 2 dolara.

⚡ Odogovor na tri moguća rešenja velikog problema povećanja ljudske energije leži u tri reči: hrana, mir, rad... Hrana za povećanje mase, mir da bi se umanjila sila nazadovanja, i rad da poveća snagu koja ubrzava ljudski napredak.

# Radio

⚡ Znam da sam njegov otac, ali meni se ne sviđa. To je neprijatnost. Nikad ga ne slušam. Radio odvlači pažnju i sprečava vas da se koncentrišete.

# Rat

⚡ Nasledio sam od svog oca, učenog čoveka koji je naporno radio za mir, neotuđivu mržnju prema ratu.

⚡ Iz ovog rata, najvećeg od početka istorije, mora se roditi novi svet, svet koji bi opravdao žrtve koje je čovečanstvo dalo. Ovaj novi svet mora biti svet u kome neće biti eksploatacije slabih od strane jakih, dobra od strane zla; gde neće biti poniženja siromašnih nasiljem bogatih; gde će proizvodi intelekta, nauke i umetnosti služiti društvu za poboljšanje i ulepšavanje života, a ne pojedincima za postizanje bogatstva. Ovaj novi svet neće biti svet potlačenih i poniženih, već slobodnih ljudi i slobodnih nacija, jednakih u dostojanstvu i poštovanju čoveka.

# Razum

⚡ Kako smo stariji, razum utvrđuje sebe i postaje sve sistematičniji i konstruktivniji.

# Roboti

⚡ U dvadeset prvom veku, robot će zauzeti mesto koje je rad robova imao u drevnoj civilizaciji.

# Religija

⚡ Nema sukoba između ideje religije i ideje nauke, ali se nauka suprotstavlja teološkim dogmama jer je zasnovana na činjenicama.

# Rotaciono polje

⚡ Ne bih dao svoje otkrice rotirajućeg polja za hiljadu drugih pronalazaka, koliko god vrednih ... Hiljadu godina nakon što telefon i video kamera zastare, princip rotacionog magnetnog polja će ostati bitan, od životne važnosti za sva buduća vremena.

# Rušenje

⚡ Stvoriti neku značajnu silu postaje sve teže svakim danom. Obrana je u stalnoj borbi sa napadom koji je u prednosti dok napreduje sa sotonskom rušilackom naukom.

⚡ Mi gradimo, ali da bi rušili. Većina našeg rada i resursa je protraćena. Naš napredak je obeležen uništenjem. Svuda je prisutan strašan gubitak vremena, napora i života. Neveseo pogled, ali istinit.

# Samokontrola

⚡ Pobedio sam svoju slabost i osetio zadovoljstvo koje nikad ranije nisam imao — da radim ono što hoću.

# Sijalica

⚡ Predviđam da će uskoro zastarela sijalica sa žarnom niti, koja ima žarulju koja se zagreje do usijanja prolazom električne struje kroz nju, potpuno nestati.

# Siromaštvo

⚡ Ako želimo smanjiti siromaštvo i bedu, ako želimo svakom zaslužnom pojedincu dati ono što je potrebno za sigurnu egzistenciju jednog inteligentnog bića, moramo obezbediti više mašina, više struje. Struja je naš oslonac, primarni izvor naših mnogobrojnih energija.

# Sloboda

⚡ Velika većina ljudskih bića nije dovoljno uvidjajna da shvati da živi u iluziji savršenog izbora i slobode u njihovim mislima i delovanjima.

# Snovi

⚡ Jednog dana, ali ne u ovom trenutku, objaviću nešto o čemu nikad nisam ni sanjao.

# Spasenje

⚡ Jedino sopstveni napori dovode do spasenja.

# Srbi

⚡ Teško da postoji nacija koja se srela sa tužnijom sudbinom od Srba. Od svog najvećeg sjaja, kada je carstvo obuhvatalo gotovo ceo severni deo balkanskog poluostrva i veliki deo onoga što je sada Austrija, srpski narod je pao u užasno ropstvo, nakon sudbonosne bitke 1389. godine na Kosovu Polju, protiv nezadrživih azijskih hordi. Evropa nikada ne može da vrati veliki dug koji duguje Srbima zbog toga što su zaustavili, žrtvovanjem sopstvene slobode, taj varvarski pohod.

⚡ Ako budem imao sreće da realizujem barem neke od mojih ideja, to će biti dobro za celo čovečanstvo. Ako se ostvare ove nade, najslađa misao će mi biti da je to delo jednog srbina.

# Strahote

⚡ Možda doživite ljudske strahote koje su van vašeg razumevanja.

# Strpljenje

⚡ Da sam probao svaku grubu ideju čim mi prvi put dođe na pamet, mogao sam da "razbijem" dve banke svaki dan. To je problem sa mnogim pronalazačima; nedostaje im strpljenje. Nedostaje im spremnost da polako i jasno rade na nečem u svom umu, kako bi zapravo "osetili da to funkcioniše". Oni žele da odmah iskoriste svoju prvu ideju; a rezultat je da koriste puno novca i puno dobrog materijala, samo da na kraju shvate da rade u pogrešnom pravcu. Svi pravimo greške, a bolje ih je napraviti pre nego što i počnemo.

# Sudbina

⚡ Dok prelistavam događaje iz mog ranijeg života shvatam koliko su suptilni uticaji koji oblikuju naše sudbine.

# Svemir

⚡ Smatram da taj prostor ne može biti zakrivljen, iz jednostavnog razloga što ne može imati svojstva.

⚡ Reći da u prisustvu velikih tela svemir postaje zakrivljen jednak je tvrdnji da nešto može da deluje na ništa.

⚡ Jedna misao može odrediti kretanje svemira.

⚡ Svako živo biće je motor usmeren na rad svemira. Iako nas naizgled pogađa samo naše neposredno okruženje, sfera spoljnog uticaja se proteže do beskonačne udaljenosti.

⚡ Kad bi samo znali veličanstvenost brojeva 3, 6 i 9, onda bi imali ključ svemira.

⚡ Ako želite da pronađete tajne svemira, mislite o energiji, frekvenciji i vibracijama.

⚡ Moj mozak je samo prijemnik, u svemiru postoji jezgro iz kojeg dobijamo znanje, snagu i inspiraciju. Nisam ušao u tajne ovog jezgra, ali znam da postoji.

⚡ Za mene, svemir je jednostavno velika mašina koja nikada nije nastala i nikada neće nestati.

# Telefon

⚡ Kada se bežična mreža savršeno primeni, čitava zemlja će se pretvoriti u ogroman mozak, čime će zapravo sve čestice postati jedna stvarna i ritmička celina. Ostvarićemo trenutnu komunikaciju, bez obzira na daljinu. I ne samo to, već ćemo putem televizije i telefona, videti i čuti jedni druge savršeno kao da smo licem u lice, uprkos medjusobne udaljenosti od hiljadu milja; a instrumenti pomoću kojih ćemo to učiniti će biti neverovatno jednostavni u poređenju sa našim sadašnjim telefonom. Čovek će biti u mogućnosti da ga nosi u svom prsluku.

⚡ Sa ovim razvojem imamo sve razloge da predvidimo da će se u vremenu koje nije tako daleko većina telegrafskih poruka preko okeana prenositi bez kablova. Za kratke daljine potreban je "bežični" telefon koji ne zahteva stručne operatere.

# Tomas Edison

⚡ Edison je bio daleko najuspešniji i verovatno, posljednji eksponent čisto empirijske metode istraživanja. Sve što je postigao bilo je rezultat upornih ispitivanja i eksperimenata koji su se često izvodili nasumce, ali uvijek potvrđujući izuzetnu snagu i bogatstvo.

⚡ Imao je pravi prezir prema učenju iz knjiga i znanju matematike, potpuno se pouzdajući u svoj istraživački instinkt i američki smisao za praksu. S obzirom na to, zaista ogromna količina njegovih stvarnih dostignuća je skoro čudo.

⚡ Njegovo postojanje je bilo sastavljeno od alternativnih perioda rada i sna u laboratoriji. Nije imao nikakav hobi, nije ga interesovao nikakav sport ili zabava bilo koje vrste i živeo je krajnje zanemarujući najosnovnija pravila higijene.

⚡ On će zauzeti jedinstvenu i uzvišenu poziciju u istoriji svoje rodne zemlje, koja bi mogla biti ponosna na njegov veliki genij i besmrtna dostignuća u interesu čovečanstva.

⚡ U njegovom umu dominirala je jedna ideja, da ne ostavi nijedan kamen netaknut, da iscrpi svaku mogućnost.

⚡ Bio sam zadivljen ovim čovekom, koji je bez temeljnog obrazovanja ili naučnog iskustva učinio toliko.

⚡ Da je trebao da nađe iglu u plastu sena, on ne bi zastao da razmisli gde je najvjerovatnije da će ona biti, već bi odmah nastavio sa grozničavom marljivošću pčele, i pregledao slamku po slamku dok ne bi našao ono što je tražio.

⚡ Samo malo teorije i proračuna bi mu spasilo devedeset posto njegovog rada.

⚡ Jedan od velikih događaja u mom životu bio je moj prvi susret sa Edisonom. Ovaj divni čovek, koji nije imao nikakvo naučno obrazovanje, a ipak je postigao toliko toga, ispunio me čuđenjem.

## Ukus

⚡ Kada spustim male kvadrate papira u posudu sa tečnošću, ja uvek osetim neobičan i užasan ukus u mojim ustima.

## Um

⚡ Čovek mora biti umeren i kontrolisati svoja čula i sklonosti na svaki način, čuvajući tako mladost svog tela i uma.

⚡ Krajnja svrha je potpuno ovladavanje uma nad materijalnim svetom, korišćenje prirode za ljudske potrebe.

⚡ Um je oštriji i jači kada je usamljen i neuznemiravan, sam sa sobom. Nije potrebna velika laboratorija da bi se razmišljalo. Originalnost se postiže kada nas ostave na miru i kada smo slobodni od spoljnih uticaja koji nas uznemiravaju i remete naš kreativni um.

⚡ Jedan slučaj može ilustrovati koliko je bio izuzetan moj život... [kao mladić] bio sam fasciniran opisom Nijagarinih vodopada, o kojima sam razmišljao i u mojoj mašti video veliki točak koji oni pokreću. Rekao sam svom ujaku da ću otići u Ameriku i sprovesti to u delo. Trideset godina kasnije video sam svoje ideje ispunjene na Nijagari i čudio se neshvatljivoj misteriji uma.

# Uspeh

⚡ Svaki napor pod pritiskom zahteva žrtvovanje životne energije.

⚡ Ako bi me ikada obuzdala sumnja u krajnji uspeh, odbacio bih je setivši se reči velikog filozofa, gospodina Kelvina, koji mi je nakon sto je prisustvovao nekim od mojih eksperimenata sa suzama u očima rekao: 'Siguran sam da ćete uspeti.'

⚡ Bio je to umetnik koji je probudio taj široki filantropski duh koji je čak i u starom veku, sjajan u učenjima plemenitih reformatora i filozofa, taj duh koji utiče na ljude u svim sferama i pozicijama da ne rade toliko za materijalnu korist ili kompenzaciju — iako i to može biti razlog — već uglavnom zbog samog uspeha, jer je zadovoljstvo postići to za dobro drugih ljudi. Kroz svoj uticaj, ti ljudi sada guraju napred, podstaknuti dubokom ljubavlju prema njihovim studijama, ljudi koji čine čuda u svojim granama, čiji je glavni cilj i uživanje sticanje i širenje znanja, ljudi koji gledaju daleko iznad zemaljskih stvari, čiji je baner Ekcelsior! Gospodo, hajde da odamo čast umetniku; Hajde da mu zahvalimo, popijmo u njegovo zdravlje!

⚡ Moj projekat je bio ograničen zakonima prirode. Svet nije bio spreman za to. Bio je mnogo pre vremena. Ali isti zakoni će prevladati i na kraju će to biti trijumfalni uspeh.

⚡ Još od detinjstva sam bio primoran da koncentrišem svoju pažnju na sebe. To mi je donelo puno patnje ali gledano iz sadašnje perspektive bila je to sreća u nesreći koja me je naučila da vrednujem nemerljivu vrednost pogleda u sebe i očuvanja života, kao i sredstvo za uspeh.

# Vanzemaljski život

⚡ Sigurno da neke planete nisu naseljene, ali druge jesu, i među njima mora postojati život u svim uslovima i fazama razvoja.

⚡ Ako postoje inteligentni stanovnici Marsa ili bilo koje druge planete, čini mi se da možemo učiniti nešto za privučemo njihovu pažnju... Razmatrao sam ovu mogućnost nekih pet ili šest godina.

⚡ Moje uvo je jedva uhvatilo signale koji dolaze u redovnim intervalima i koji se nisu mogli proizvesti na Zemlji.

⚡ Mora da postoji život na drugim planetama. Sunce sija. Zvezde odaju toplotu. Voda se skuplja na površini. Pojavljuju se hemijske promene koje još ne razumemo — i postaje život.

# Veštačka inteligencija

⚡ Mogu se napraviti mašine koje će raditi kao da imaju razum, ograničenog obima, i one će napraviti revoluciju u mnogim ekonomskim i industrijskim oblastima.

# Volja

⚡ Čovek se ne može spasti od svojih ludosti ili poroka tuđim naporima ili protestima, već samo upotrebom svoje sopstvene volje.

# Zemlja

⚡ Zemlja može da eksplodira. Neka planeta može da se sudari sa nama. Ali bez obzira, zemlja postoji već veoma dugo.

⚡ Od velikog značaja bi bilo znati koji je kapacitet zemlje i koji je njen napon ako bi bila naelektrisana.

⚡ Ideja me je postepeno obuzimala da se zemlja može koristiti umesto žice, tako da se potpuno izuzmu veštački provodnici. Ogromna veličina zemlje je izgledala kao nepremostiva prepreka, ali nakon dužeg proučavanja ovog predmeta postao sam uveren da je poduhvat moguć.

## Zapažanje

⚡ Nedovoljno posmatranje je samo je oblik neznanja, uzrok mnogih perverznih incidenata i trijumfa ludih ideja.

## Znanje

⚡ Sva znanja ili koncepti se zapažaju kroz medijum oka, bilo kao odgovor na direktan stimulus mrežnjače ili slabije sekundarne efekte i odjeke. Drugi organi čula mogu samo izazvati osećaje koji nemaju stvarnost postojanja i od kojih se ne mogu formirati nikakvi koncepti.

⚡ Ako bi neki genijalni izum sutra otkrio tajnu besmrtnosti, večne lepote i mladosti za kojim celo čovečanstvo boluje, isti neumoljivi agenti koji sprečavaju mnoštvo da iznenada promijeni brzinu, također će se odupreti snazi novog znanja sve dok vreme postepeno ne promeni ljudsku misao.

⚡ Opasnost od sukoba povećava se opasno zbog više ili manje dominantnog osećaja ratobornosti koja je prisutna u svakom ljudskom biću. Najbolji način da se suprotstavimo ovoj tendenciji jeste raspršivanje neznanja sistematskim širenjem opšteg znanja. Imajući ovo na umu, najvažnija je pomoć kroz razmenu mišljenja i odnosa.

# Želja

⚡ Kada se prirodna sklonost razvije u strastvenu želju, napredak ka svom cilju ide koracima od sedam milja.

# Žene

⚡ Žene neće postići svoju jednakost i kasnije svoju superiornosti zbog površnog fizičkog imitiranja muškaraca, već zbog buđenju intelekta žena.

# Život

⚡ Život je bio neizbežan.

⚡ Život jeste i uvek će ostati nerešiva jednačina, ali on ipak sadrži određene poznate faktore.

⚡ Mišljenje sveta ne utiče na mene. Stavio sam kao prave vrednosti u svom životu ono što će ostati nakon što umrem.

⚡ Od svih beskrajno raznovrsnih fenomena koje priroda predstavlja našim čulima, ne postoji nijedan koji ispunjava naš um većim čudom od onog nepojmljivo složenog pokreta koji označavamo kao ljudski život. Njegovo misteriozno poreklo je skriveno u zauvek neprohodnoj magli prošlosti, njegov karakter je postao nerazumljiv svojom beskonačnom složenošću, a njegova destinacija je skrivena u beskrajnim dubinama budućnosti.

⚡ Čak i neorganska materija, ona koja se smatra mrtvom, reaguje na nevernike i daje nepobitan dokaz principa života u sebi. Sve što postoji, organsko ili neorgansko, živo i neživo je osetljivo na spoljne stimulanse.

⚡ Potičem iz vrlo žilave i dugotrajne rase. Neki od mojih predaka su stogodišnjaci, a jedan od njih je živeo 129 godina. Odlučan sam da održim tu tradiciju i sebi pružim zadovoljstvo sa perspektivom velikog obećanja. Mada opet, priroda mi je dala živopisnu maštu.

# Index

# Indeks

# About the author

***Dobrica Savić*** is a conference speaker, presenter, moderator, writer, editor, manager, digital transformation enthusiast, chair of international committees, life-long learner and avid knowledge seeker. He has specialized in in the field of information and knowledge organization, working for various United Nations agencies and organizations for over 30 years. He holds a Doctorate degree from Middlesex University in London, an MPhil in Information Science from Loughborough University, UK, an MA in International Relations from the University of Belgrade, Serbia, and a Graduate Diploma in Public Administration, Concordia University, Montreal, Canada. He has published few books, written over 50 articles, and presented at over 30 international conferences on various subjects. He enjoys reading, writing, and collecting and organizing sayings, quotes and wisdoms.

# O autoru

***Dobrica Savić*** je učesnik na konferencijama, predavač, moderator, pisac, urednik, menadžer, entuzijast digitalne transformacije, predsedavajući međunarodnih komiteta, doživotni student i strastveni tragač za znanjem. Specijalizirao se u oblasti organizacije informacija i znanja, radeći za različite agencije i organizacije Ujedinjenih nacija više od 30 godina. Doktorirao je na Middlesex univerzitetu u Londonu, magistrirao informatiku na Loughborough univerzitetu u Velikoj Britaniji, magistrirao međunarodne odnose na Univerzitetu u Beogradu, Srbija, i specijalizirao javnu upravu, na Concordia univerzitetu u Montrealu, Kanada. Objavio je nekoliko knjiga, napisao preko 50 članaka i drzao prezentacije na različite tcme na preko 30 medunarodnih konferencija. On uživa u čitanju, pisanju i sakupljanju i organizovanju izreka, citata i mudrosti.

www.ingramcontent.com/pod-product-compliance
Lightning Source LLC
Chambersburg PA
CBHW020321290526
45785CB00007B/2875